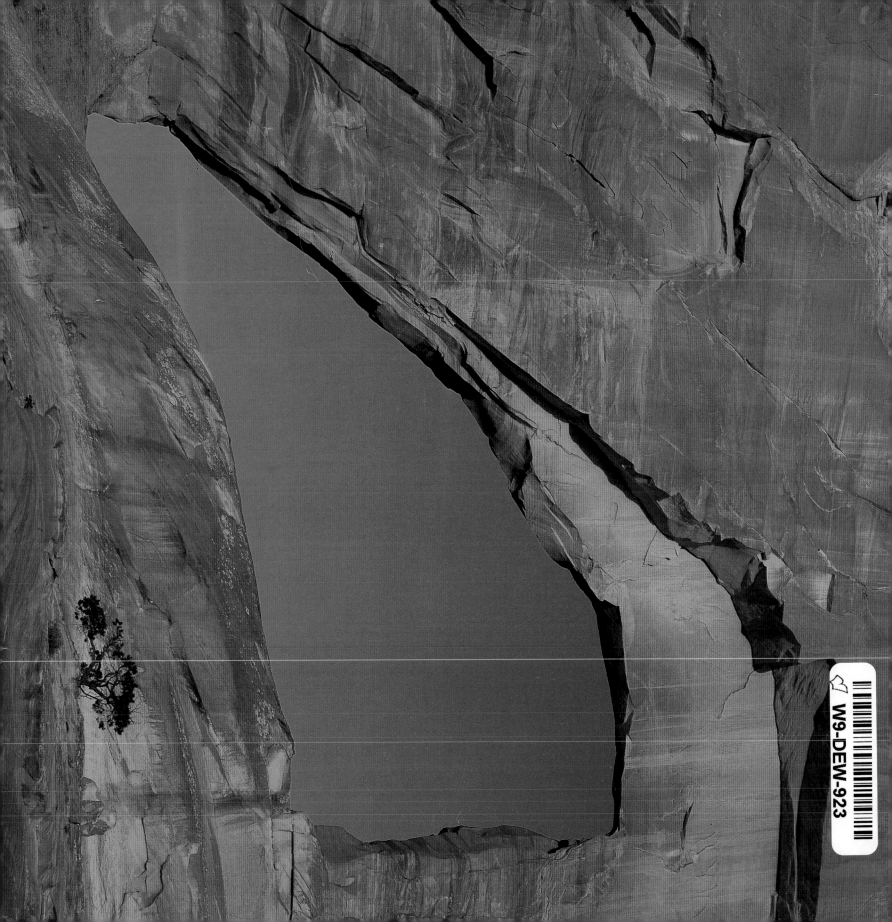

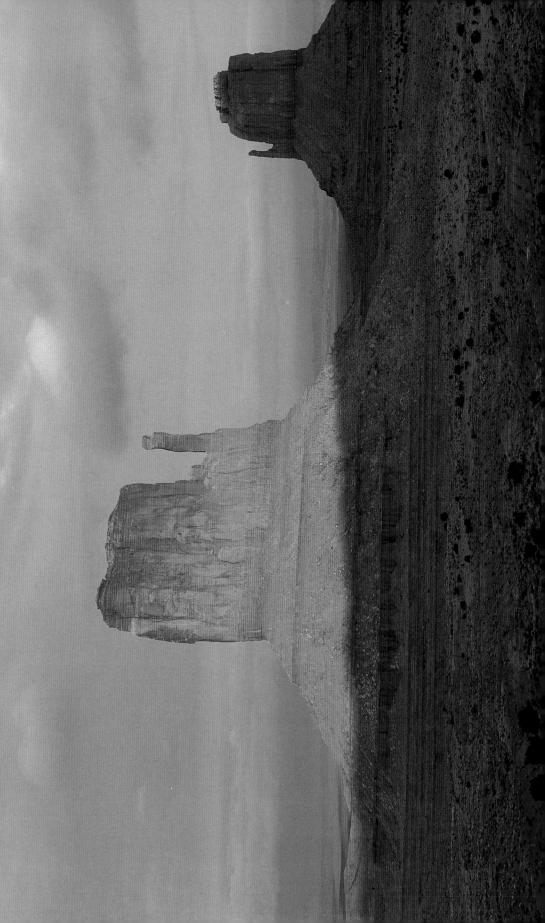

THE WOVEN SPIRIT

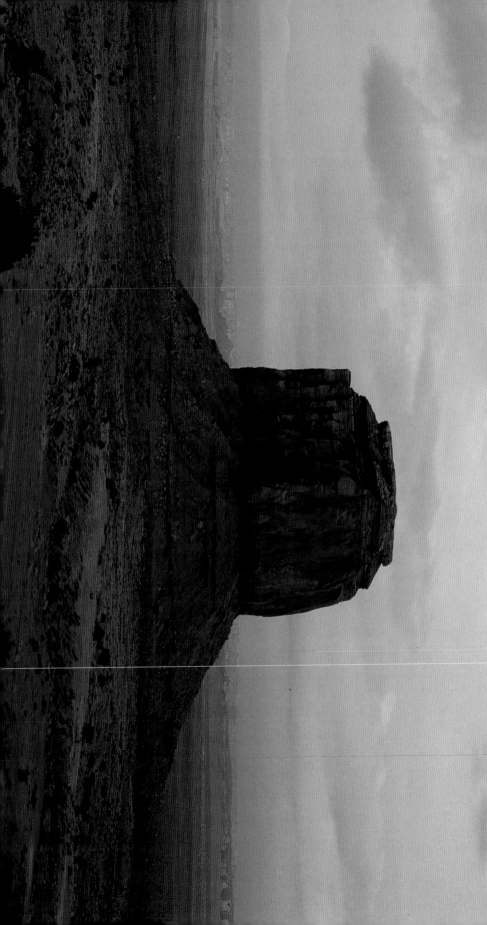

OF THE SOUTHWEST

BY DON AND DEBRA MCQUISTON

WITH TEXT BY LYNNE BUSH AND PHOTOGRAPHY BY TOM TILL

CHRONICLE BOOKS
SAN FRANCISCO

Library of Congress Cataloging-in-Publication Data available.

McQuiston, Don.

The woven spirit of the Southwest / by Don and Debra McQuiston, text by Lynne Bush, with photography by Tom Till.

p. cm.

Includes bibliographical references.

ISBN 0-8118-0864-5 (HC)

ISBN 0-8118-0880-7 (PB)

1. Indian textile fabrics—Southwest, New.
2. Southwest. New—Pictorial works.
3. Indians of North America—Southwest, New.

I. McQuiston, Debra.
II. Bush, Lynne.
III. Till, Tom.

E78.S7M18   1996

746.1'4'089974079—dc20   95-7347
                                              CIP

Printed in Hong Kong

Distributed in Canada by Raincoast Books
8680 Cambie Street
Vancouver, British Columbia V6P 6M9

10 9 8 7 6 5 4 3 2 1

Chronicle Books
275 Fifth Street
San Francisco, California 94103

Page 1: White Mesa Arch, Arizona
Page 2-3: Monument Valley Navajo Tribal Park

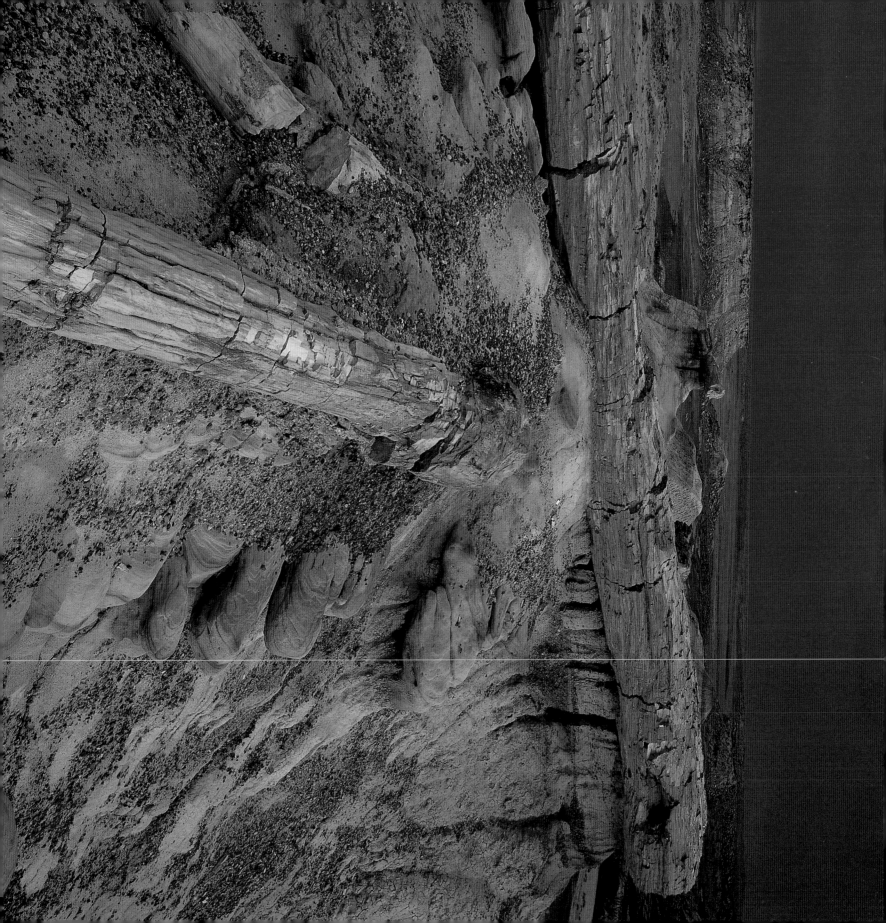

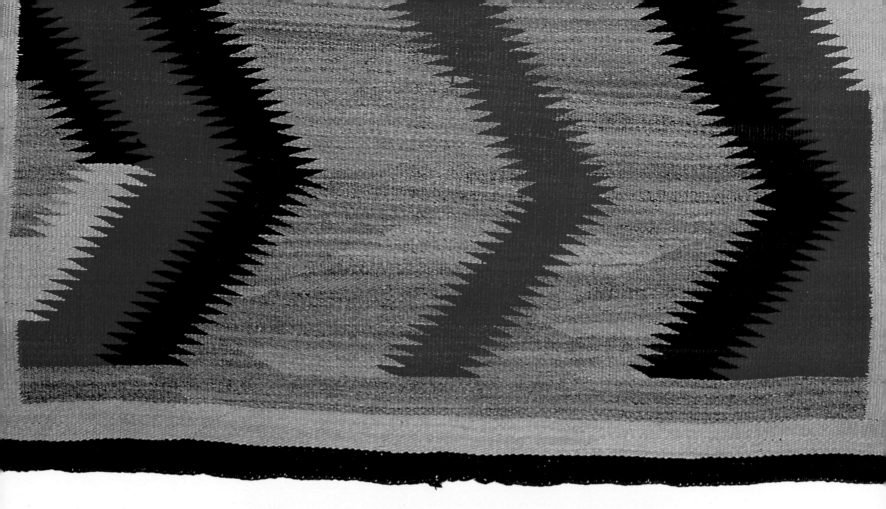

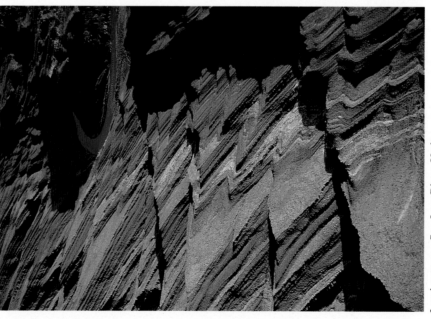

Land patterns, San Juan River, Utah

Rug, early 1900s, courtesy San Diego Museum of Man

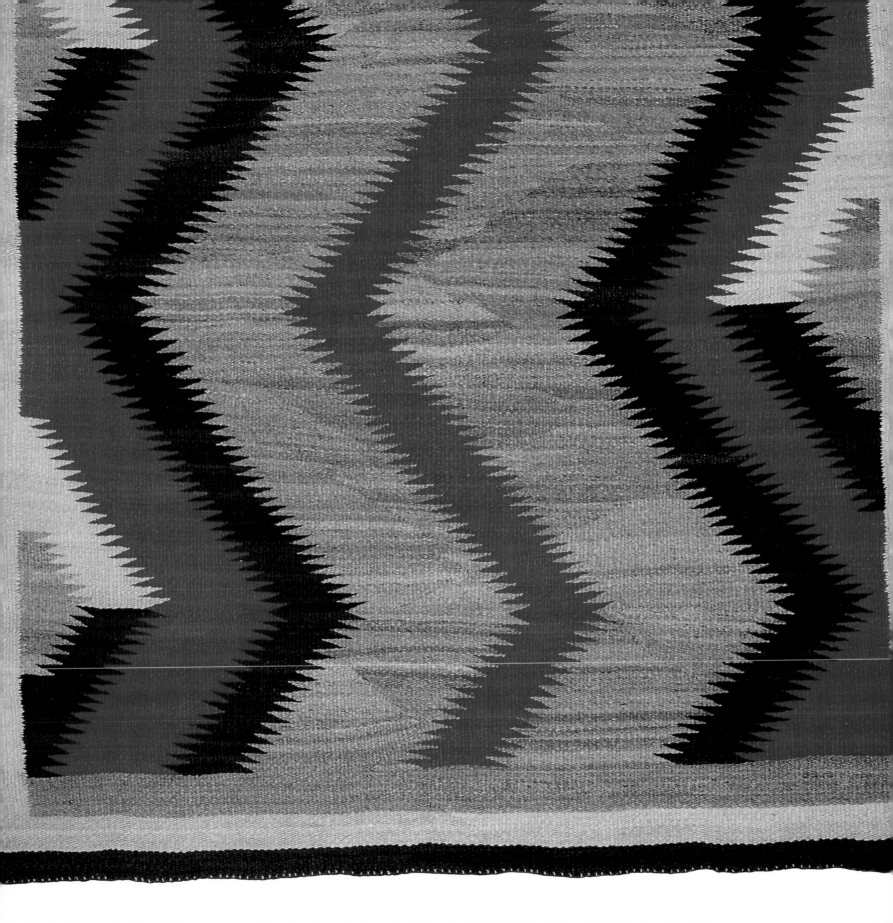

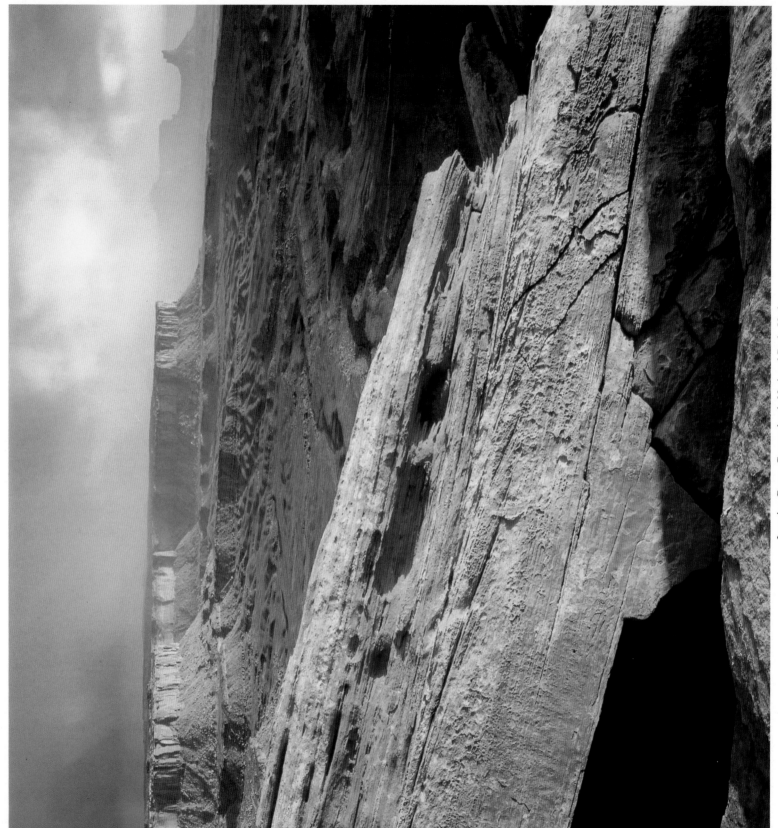

Junction Butte, Canyonlands National Park, Utah

CONTENTS

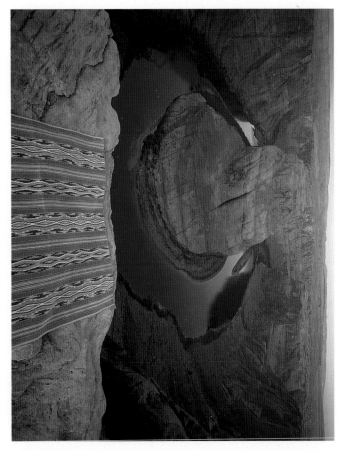

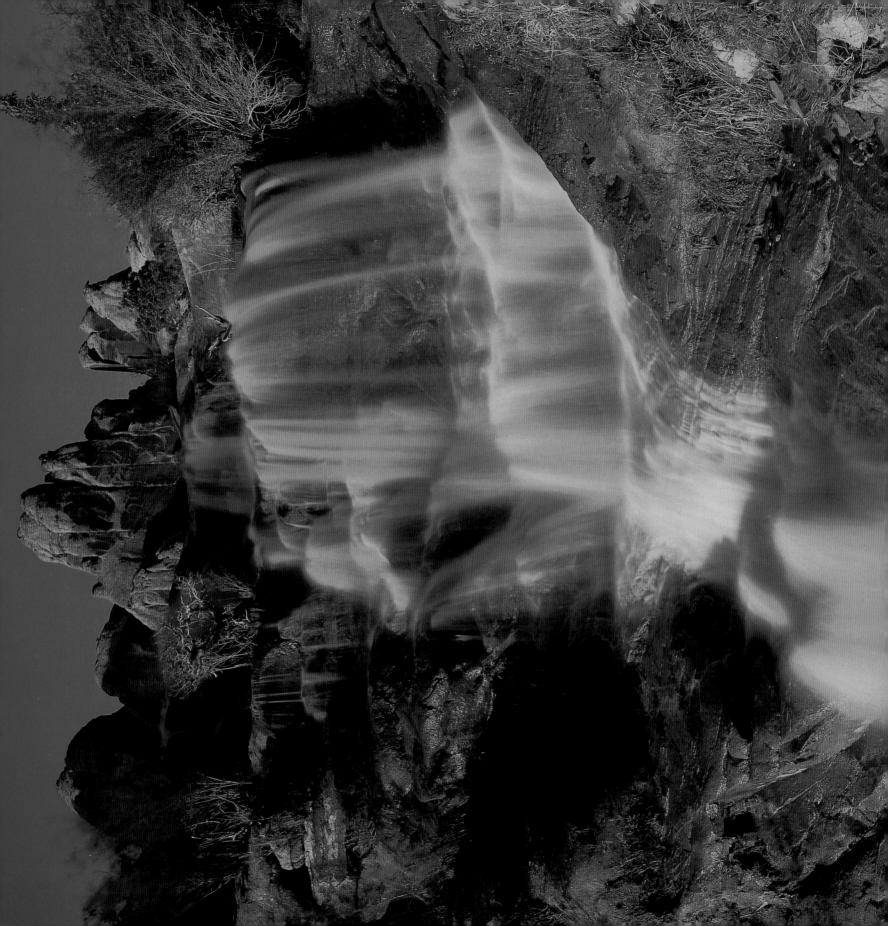

IT BEGINS

WITH WATER

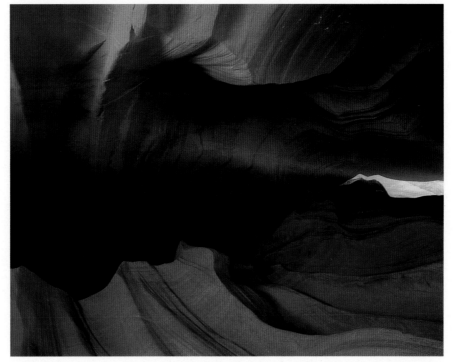

Flash flood near La Sal Mountains, Utah
Above: Slot canyon, Colorado Plateau, Arizona

IT BEGINS WITH WATER

Rocks, as far as the eye can see. It's dusty, hot, and dry. So dry it seems it must never rain here. But summer is marked by daily thunderstorms. Flash floods are common in this parched land. In no time at all a dry wash can be bank to bank in fast flowing muddy water. On the road from Cameron to Tuba City, lightning forks down on the side of the road. On the road from Kayenta to Chinle, a fierce downpour pounds the red earth to slippery clay and hangs a rainbow over the fields of Many Farms.

A marvelous contradiction. The story of this desert is a story that begins with water. Water in the form of ancient seas laid down the vast sedimentary deposits from which the Painted Desert, Monument Valley, the Grand Canyon, and others were formed. Erosion by wind and water then shaped the land, creating fantastic and bizarre sculptures, and carving great gorges and canyons.

The Colorado Plateau itself was laid down by Paleozoic seas. Hardened and compressed through time to rock, it was lifted up by tectonic forces as the Colorado and its tributaries cut down, shaping the land in a mighty clash of rock and water. The combination of these forces, of rock thrust up and water raging, scouring, cutting down, has carved the land of the Southwest. The river is old now, but still carries away a tremendous amount of material each year. Water in other forms continues its erosive work as well. Rainwater, seeping in and freezing in the inter-crystalline spaces of the rock, speeds the shearing of rock from the cliff, turning mesa into butte, butte into monument, and monument into a pile of fragments shattered at its former base, ready to be formed again into sandstone or conglomerate or metamorphosed into something harder. It's an endless cycling and recycling, a slow, creeping process that cannot be measured by the eye, by the life span of one, but only by generations.

If you had been here during the Triassic

period, some 250 million years ago, you would have been accompanied by strange creatures. The land masses of the earth were gathered together into the supercontinent Pangaea. What is now Arizona was close to the equator, giving it a tropical climate. Present-day Nevada was on the coast. You would have been on the lookout for giant meat-eating meptosaurs, crocodile-like phytosaurs, and freshwater sharks, which waited for unwary prey in warm swamps. Primitive fish like coelocanths and lungfish, still with us today, swam in the murky pools and streams lined by giant horsetails and by conifers that resembled palm trees. Gradually, as the continents moved apart and the swamps began to dry, first dinosaurs, then large mammals, roamed across the Southwest. And, if you'd been here during the Triassic you would have been the solitary member of your species. Other humans would not show up for another 230 million years.

After the swamps came a period of mountain building to the south and uplift to the north. Volcanoes became active, some exploding with thick lava and ash and some extruding a thin basaltic lava that spread for miles. Humans appeared and spread across the face of the earth. Those who first arrived in North America migrated across the Bering land bridge to what is now Alaska and then worked their way south. The Southwest still had abundant water. Prehistoric hunters swept across the area's grassy plains, hunting mammoths, mastodons, and now-extinct species of bison, horses, and camels. They left behind stone spearheads, the earliest human artifacts found here. The big-game hunters did not stay, however. The earliest permanent residents were collectors of edible roots, nuts, and wild seeds and hunters of small game such as deer and rabbit. They were nomads, traveling far and wide to take advantage of seasonal variations in food supply. Their day-to-day life was a struggle to gather enough food to survive.

Cultivation of crops that were first developed in what is now Mexico helped the nomads settle down. Remains of corn dating back to 4000 B.C. have been found in New Mexico. Other early crops included squash, kidney beans, and cotton. Farmers used a sharp, pointed stick to punch holes for the seed in small hillocks. Getting water to the crops became all-important. Some carried water by hand, first in pitch-lined baskets, later in ceramic pots. Others built elaborate irrigation systems with miles of canals, or systems of barricades to divert runoff. Crops were raised on fertile bottom land near rivers or streams.

Permanent settlements began to spring up. Pit houses were popular among many of the desert cultures. As the struggle for food became less time-consuming, other aspects of these societies began to develop. There was time to decorate pot-tery and weave cotton cloth. Religious ceremonies were created. Architecture became more elaborate, growing both upward and outward. Clusters of stone rooms, with roof beams of pine, were built both against the cliffs and as free-standing villages. The pit house style was retained in the kivas, underground rooms where ceremonies were held and secret societies met. These early people, called the Anasazi, or ancient enemies, by the Navajo, left behind many artifacts of their daily lives, preserved by the dry desert air.

The story of the Southwest, then, is the story of two titans, rock and water, locked in constant combat. Water will win; it always has, aided by wind and gravity. But rock continues to stand tall, to defy gravity in its sheer-sided cliffs, its spires and arches, its massiveness. And so, too, the people of the Southwest continue, making their way in a land of harsh and unexpected beauty.

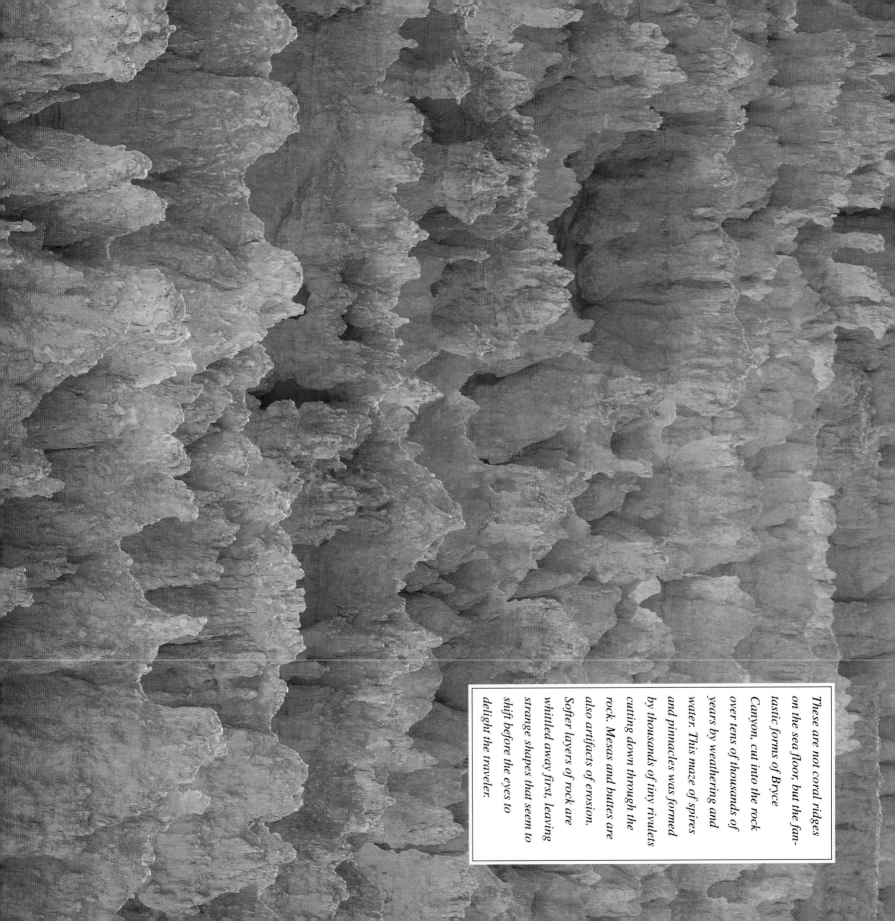

These are not coral ridges on the sea floor, but the fantastic forms of Bryce Canyon, cut into the rock over tens of thousands of years by weathering and water. This maze of spires and pinnacles was formed by thousands of tiny rivulets cutting down through the rock. Mesas and buttes are also artifacts of erosion. Softer layers of rock are whittled away first, leaving strange shapes that seem to shift before the eyes to delight the traveler.

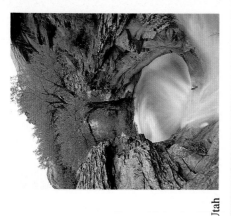

Slowly, slowly, aided by the sand and gravel it carries, water grinds down the rock. It freezes in the cracks in cliff faces, expanding, pulling molecule from molecule, weakening the rock's hold until gravity takes over and pulls it down. It tumbles and splashes from high to low, wearing the cliff face away as it falls.

Flash flood, Colorado River, Utah

Goosenecks of the San Juan River, Utah

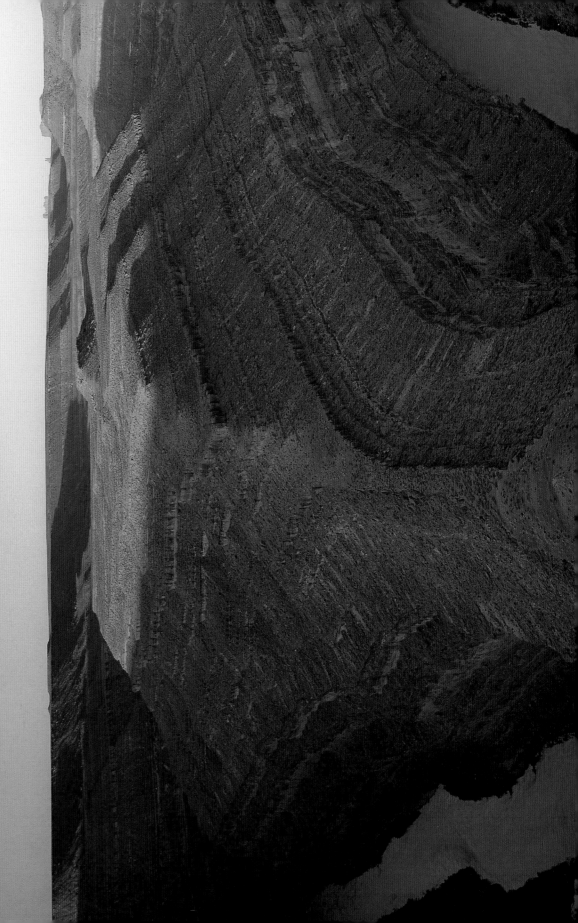

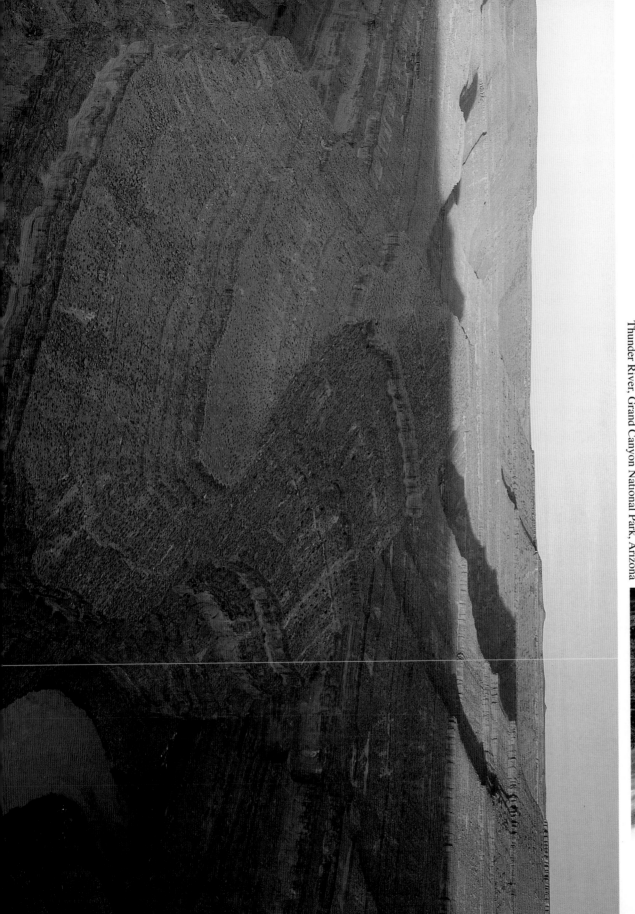

Thunder River, Grand Canyon National Park, Arizona

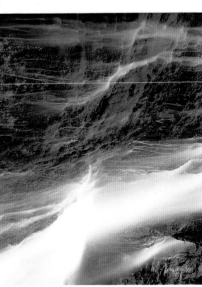

Rainwater potholes, Canyon Rims
Recreation Area, Utah

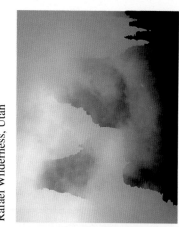

Fisher Towers in fog, Proposed San
Rafael Wilderness, Utah

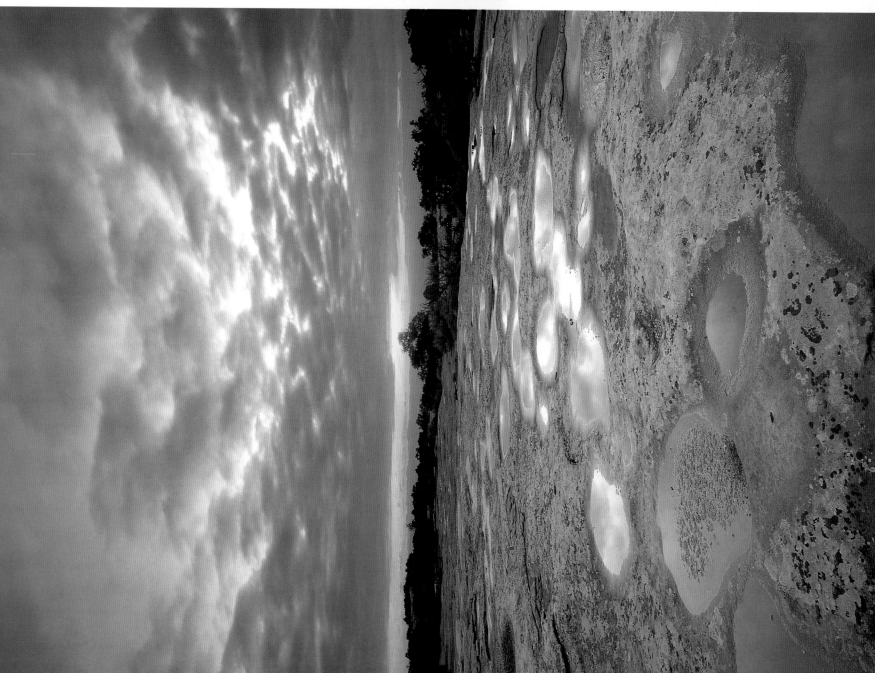

Bristlecone pine,
Ashdown Gorge
Wilderness, Utah

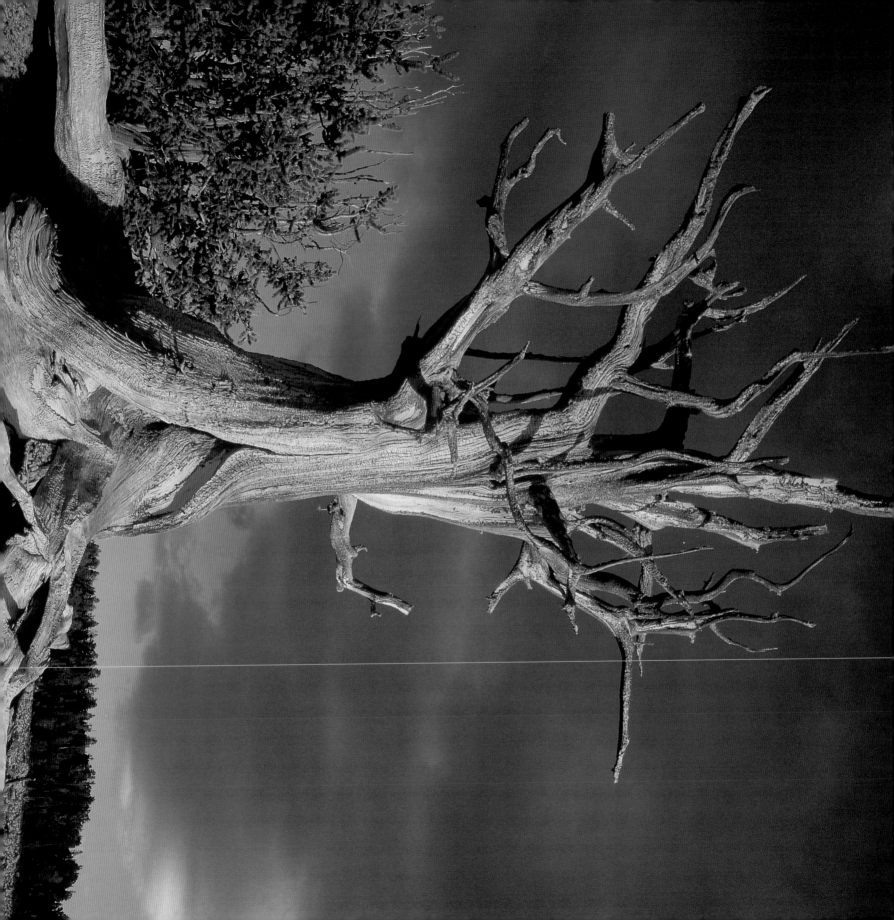

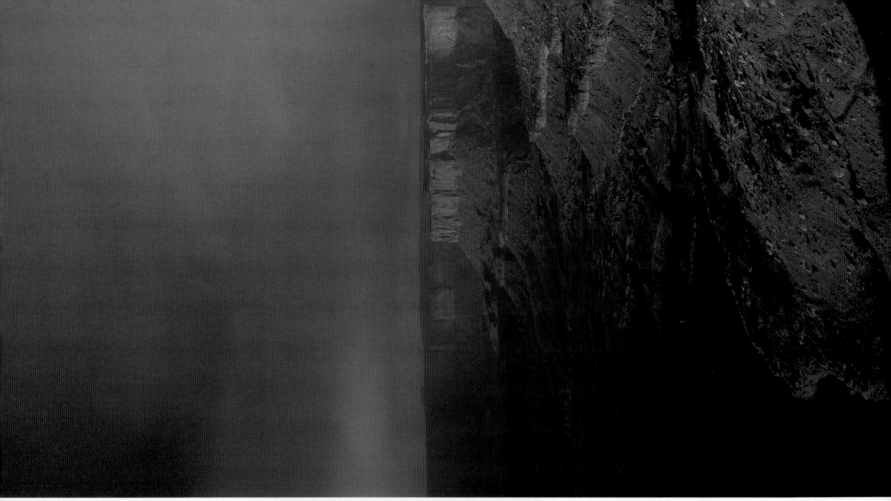

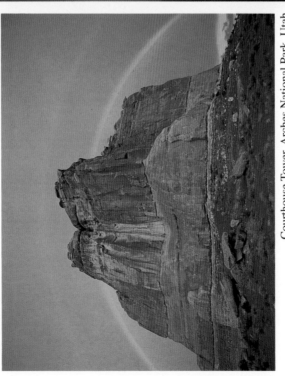

Courthouse Tower, Arches National Park, Utah

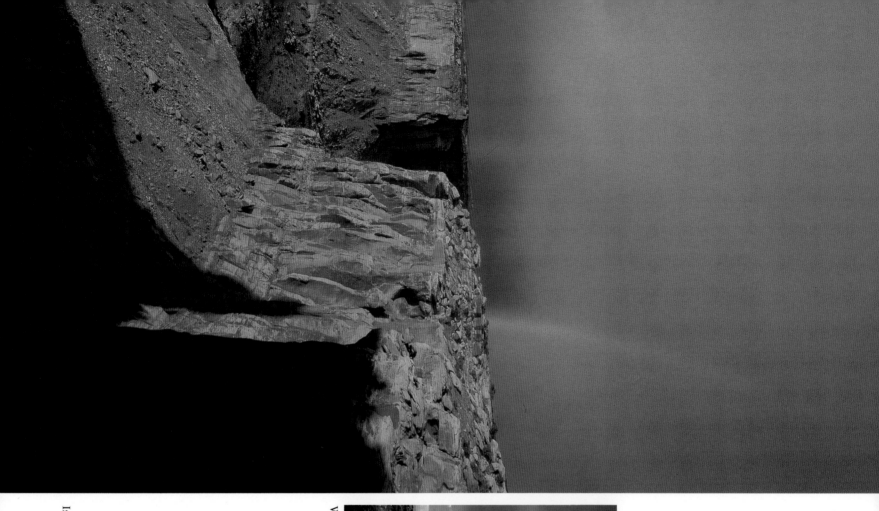

Island in the Sky, Canyonlands National Park, Utah

Wupatki National Monument, Arizona

21

THE ANCIENT ONES

Each summer, near Winslow, Arizona, archeologists and volunteers sift dirt and shovel rock all day in the blazing sun at Homol'ovi II, one of 400 archeological sites that have been identified in the area. They are searching for clues about the people who once lived here.

A walk to the current excavation site winds up a dusty pink slope through typical desert scrub. The ground is littered with potsherds—orange, gray, corrugated white, some still covered with soot from fires burned out hundreds of years ago. Several rooms have been excavated, with substantial portions of their walls below the present ground level. A sign identifies the peculiar indentations in the ground on either side of the path. Pot hunters, in search of buried treasures, have been here before the archeologists. It is hard to estimate the extent of the damage they have done.

Around the back side of the hill on which the excavation is taking place are petroglyphs, strange signs scratched into the rock by those who passed by here many centuries ago. The weathering of the rock has made many of these distinguishable only at certain angles. A certain tilt of the head reveals much that cannot be seen straight on. Fire Clan was here. Bear Clan was here, too. A recurring pattern of concentric circles is said to symbolize the wanderings of the Hopi clans before they settled around Black Mesa. The Hopi claim the peoples who lived here as Hisatsinom, or ancestors. Historical and archeological evidence seems to back up many of the stories carried forward in their oral tradition.

Tsegi Canyon, in the heart of Navajo country, was once the home of a flourishing agricultural community. Now sheep and an occasional cow roam its overgrazed flats. The hardy can hike down into the canyon with a ranger to visit the ancient homes of the Anasazi at Betatakin. The very hardy can arrange a trip to Keet Seel, a day's hike up the main fork of the canyon.

The trail begins as a dirt road, then becomes a

wide gravel path that narrows as it wanders up and down along the ridge. The descent, when it comes, is sudden and steep, about 1,500 feet in 1/2 mile. Even stairs cut into the rock by the Park Service aren't much help. At the bottom of the switchback the path to Keet Seel turns left. Betatakin travelers continue along the edge of the side valley and gradually descend into scrub pine forest. The path begins to climb again, and as it does the vegetation changes, becomes more lush. There are aspen and horsetails, and the sound of running water. The path is muddy in spots. Small lizards scuffle in the undergrowth and bees hang lazily in the warm air.

Betatakin sits at the head of the canyon, in a great arched cave of pink sandstone. The walls and rooms of the ruin blend into the back of the cave, making them appear somewhat unreal. Getting into the ruin entails a precipitous climb up a set of steps cut into the rock. At the far left edge of the cave are three perfect rooms, sealed off for

all time by an accident of erosion. To the right are a cluster of granaries, with stone metates for grinding corn and bins with stone slabs for sides still in place. The grain storage rooms have doors of a different shape from the others. A slab door fits flush to keep out rodents and other pests. Living quarters are small and cramped; many show evidence of old fires. Most activities must have been carried on out of doors, with these tiny rooms reserved for sleeping.

The walls, still standing after almost 1,000 years, were built of detritus from the cliff's weathering, shaped to rough uniformity. A crude mortar holds the stones in place. In spots the mortar has been packed with pebbles and twigs to reinforce it. The spring that supplied water to Betatakin in the Middle Ages still flows fresh and pure. The Hopi come at various times of the year to collect water from this sacred place for ceremonial use. Past the spring are pictographs, wall paintings similar to the petroglyphs at Homol'ovi.

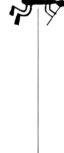

Betatakin and Keet Seel were built at about the same time and abandoned at about the same time. Each was occupied for roughly a century. Who lived at Betatakin? Why did they move so far up the valley, away from their fields? What dangers were they running from? Some have theorized that the cliff dwellers were escaping from enemies, real or imagined. Others point to evidence of a great drought and a dropping water table in the valley, making it harder to farm. Perhaps they were trying to save every scrap of river-bottom land for cultivation. Looking out from under the shelter of the great arch, another explanation comes to mind. Perhaps they were overwhelmed by the beauty of this place and could not leave it once they had found it.

Why did they finally leave? Yes, there was a drought, but long droughts had happened before. Did this one have more impact? The migration seems to have coincided with the appearance of the Kachinas, supernatural spirits who brought knowledge and help. Did the Kachinas ask the people to come to them? Whatever happened was of great significance, for it moved not only the people of Betatakin and Keet Seel, but most of the rest of the population of Tsegi Canyon as well. Indeed, there was a general migration to the south, to Homol'ovi, to Black Mesa, and to other locations and villages, now lost.

Hopi legend tells of years of wandering after humans came up through the sipapuni, the opening from the Third World into this world. Aided by Spider Grandmother and her twin grandsons, Pokanghoya and Polongahoya, the people made their way. Perhaps the abandonment of the cliff houses was foreordained. In any case, we can only guess now, can only dimly discern the shape of Anasazi life from the fragments of knowledge we hold, as the archeologist reconstructs the pot from its shards.

24

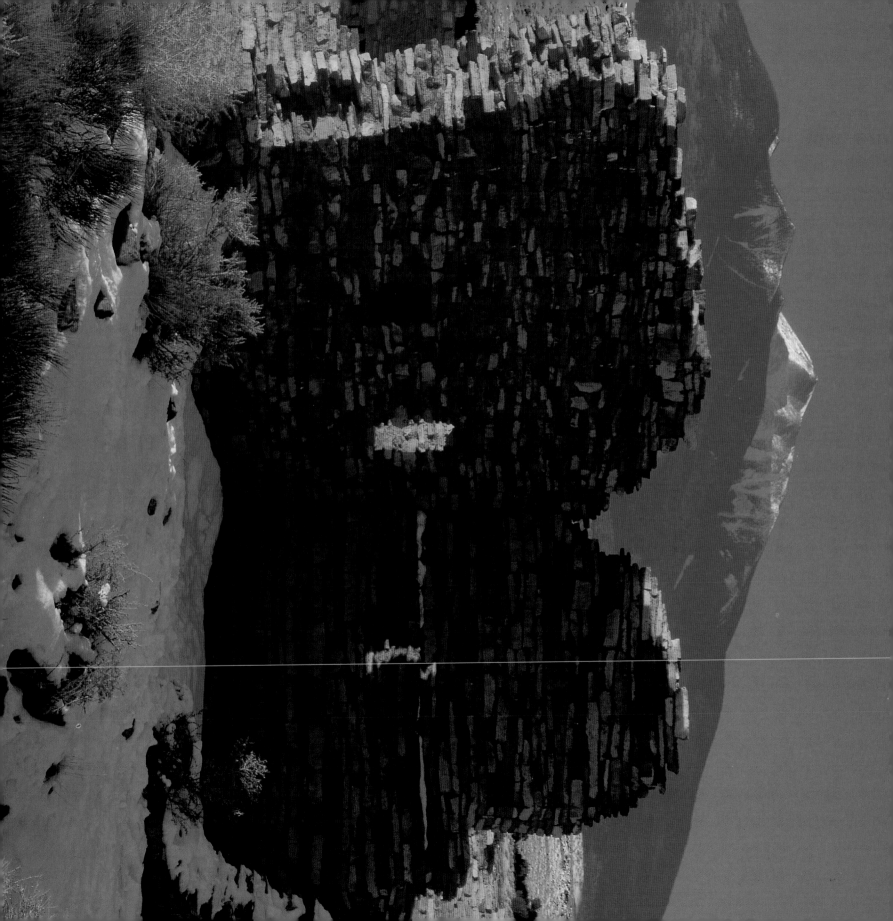

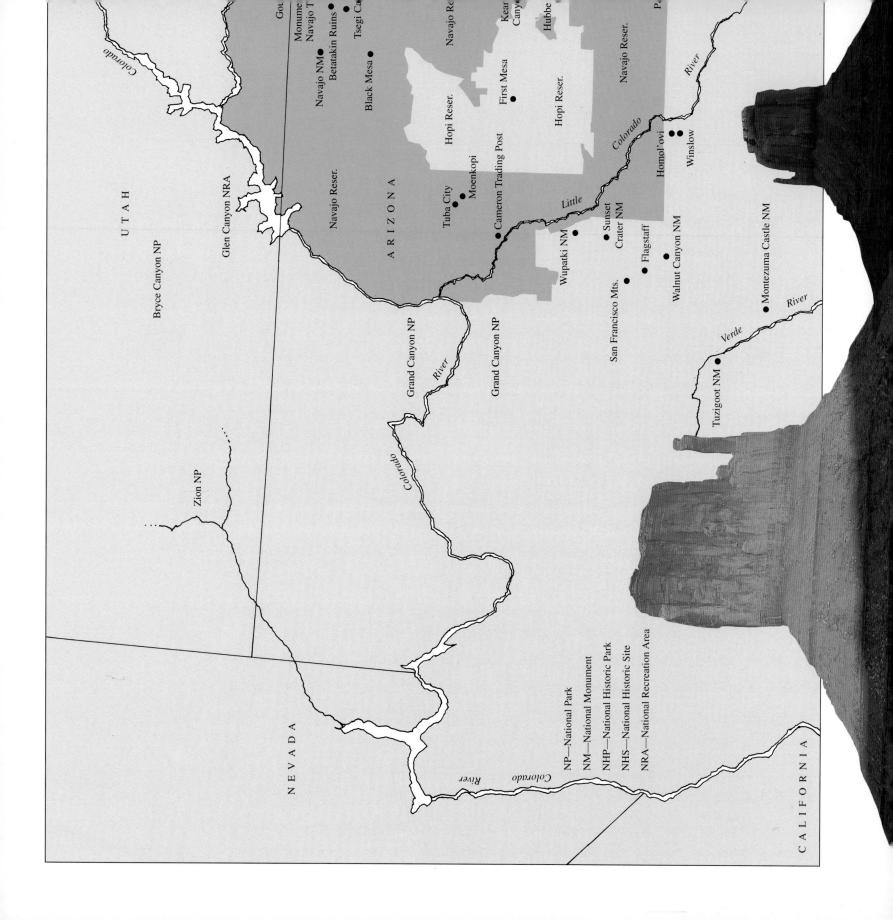

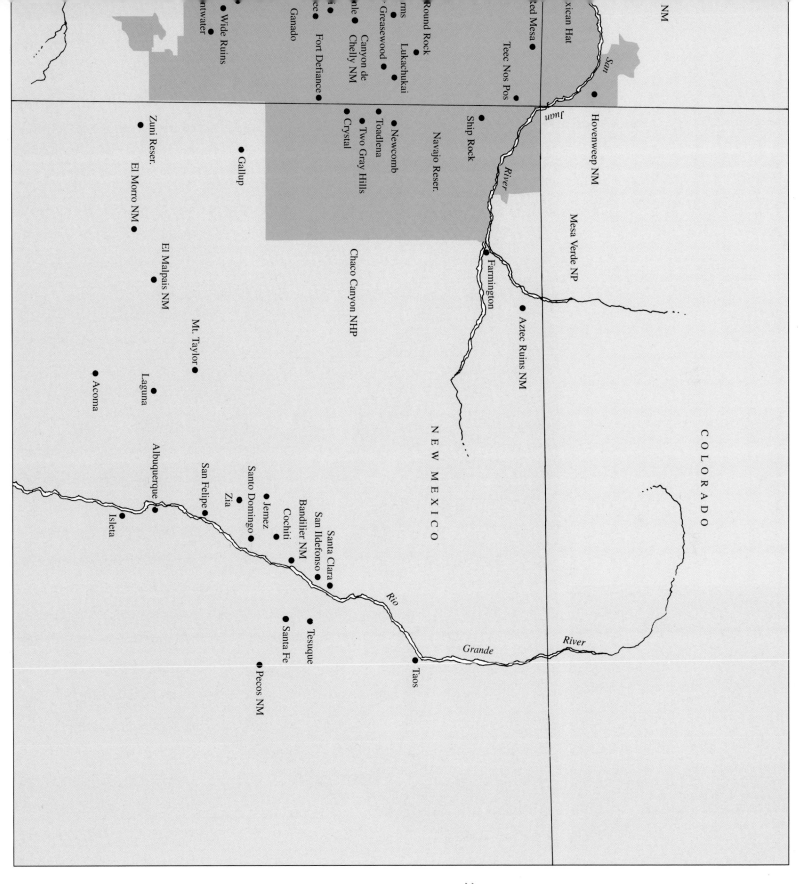

NM

San Juan River

xican Hat

Hovenweep NM

ked Mesa

Mesa Verde NP

Teec Nos Pos

Ship Rock

Navajo Reser.

Farmington

Aztec Ruins NM

Round Rock

Lukachukai

Newcomb

Toadlena

Two Gray Hills

Crystal

Greasewood

rms

Canyon de
Chelly NM

Fort Defiance

ee

Wide Ruins

ntwater

Ganado

Zuni Reser.

El Morro NM

Gallup

El Malpais NM

Mt. Taylor

Laguna

Acoma

COLORADO

N E W   M E X I C O

Chaco Canyon NHP

Albuquerque

Isleta

San Felipe

Zia

Santo Domingo

Jemez

Cochiti

Bandilier NM

San Ildefonso

Santa Clara

Tesuque

Santa Fe

Rio

Grande

River

Taos

Pecos NM

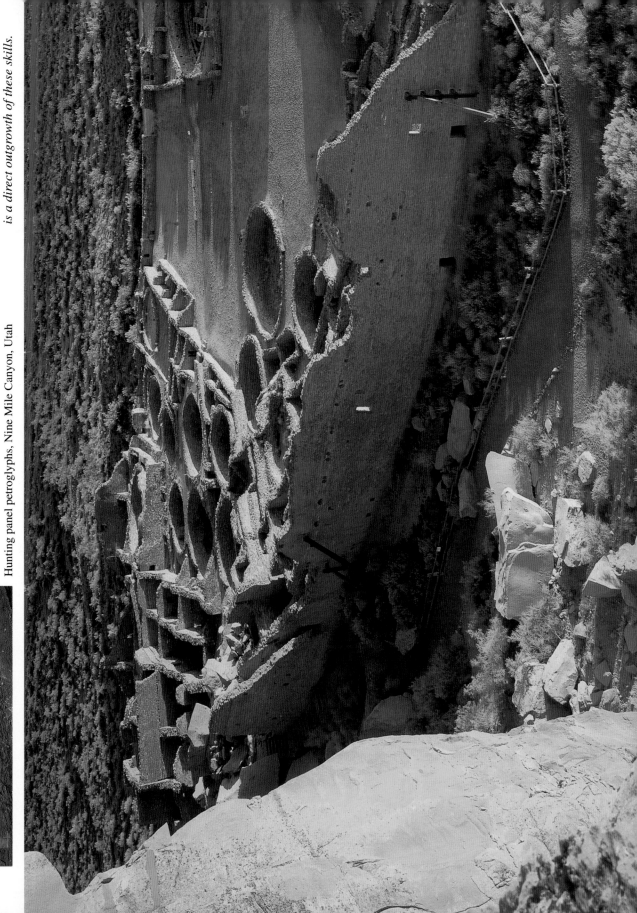

Vaguely human forms mingle with animals on the walls of Nine-Mile Canyon in Utah. The Anasazi, architects of Pueblo Bonito, Chaco Canyon, and many other sites were known as builders and farmers. They were also skilled artists, as their highly decorated pottery shows. Today's much admired Southwestern style of architecture is a direct outgrowth of these skills.

Hunting panel petroglyphs, Nine Mile Canyon, Utah

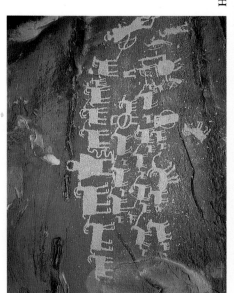

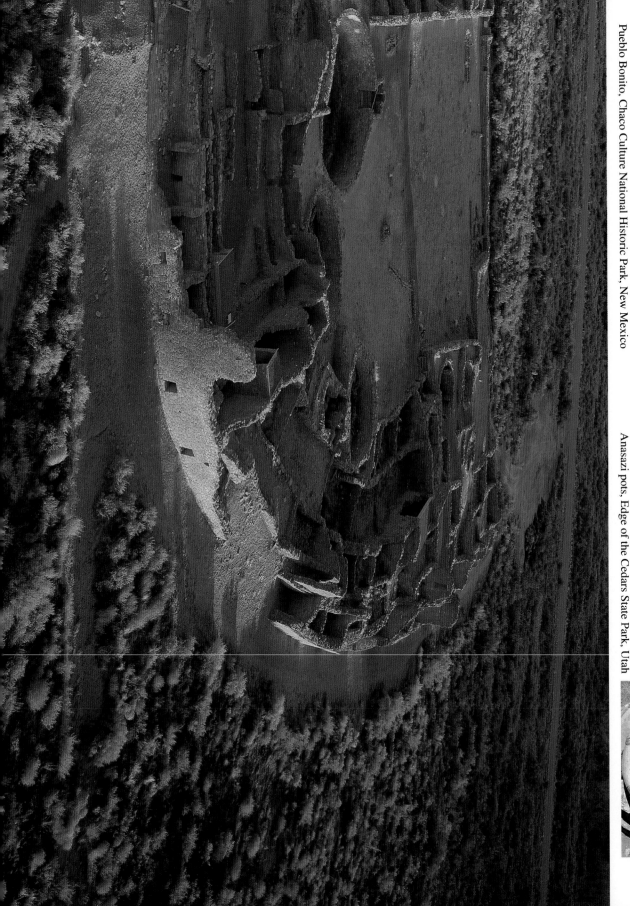

Pueblo Bonito, Chaco Culture National Historic Park, New Mexico

Anasazi pots, Edge of the Cedars State Park, Utah

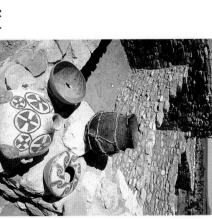

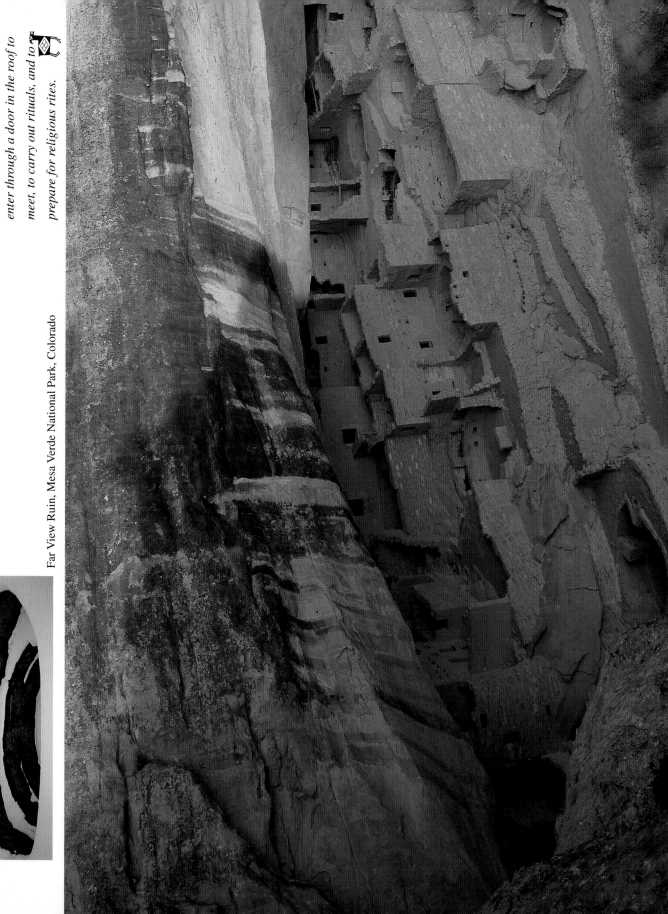

The spectacular ruins of the Cliff Palace at Mesa Verde show the distinctive remains of many large kivas, or ceremonial rooms. These round underground rooms, found at nearly every ruin site, are still a feature of modern pueblos. Initiates of the secret Kachina Societies enter through a door in the roof to meet, to carry out rituals, and to prepare for religious rites.

Far View Ruin, Mesa Verde National Park, Colorado

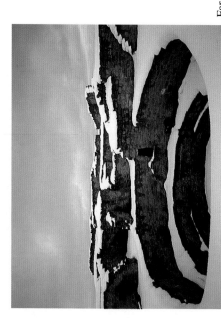

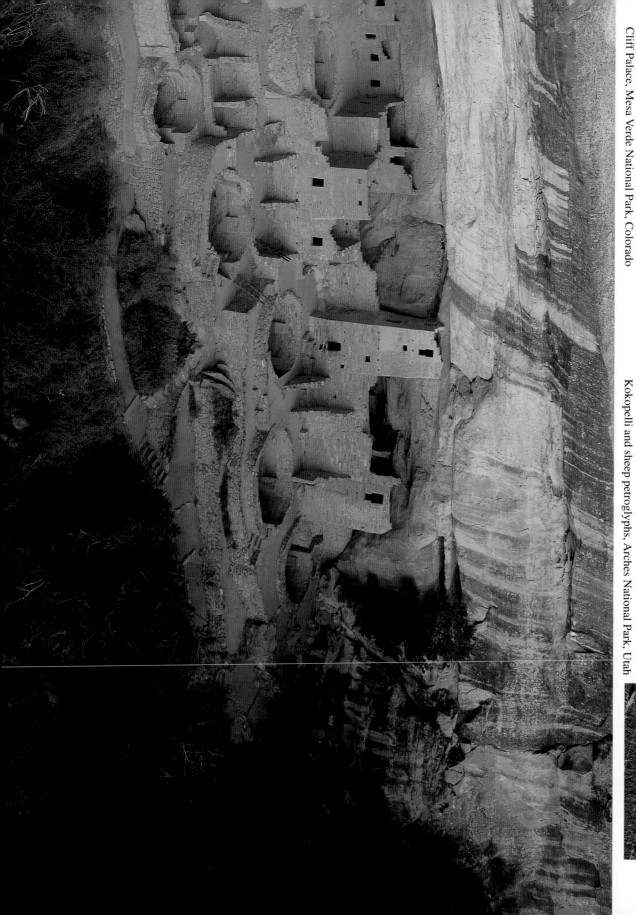

Cliff Palace, Mesa Verde National Park, Colorado

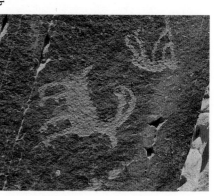

Kokopelli and sheep petroglyphs, Arches National Park, Utah

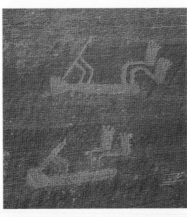

Kokopelli petroglyphs, Monument Valley Tribal Park, Arizona–Utah

Kokopelli, the flute player, graces many a canyon wall, as do long-horned sheep, scratched into the sandstone by long-vanished wanderers. The exact meaning of the figures faded away with their

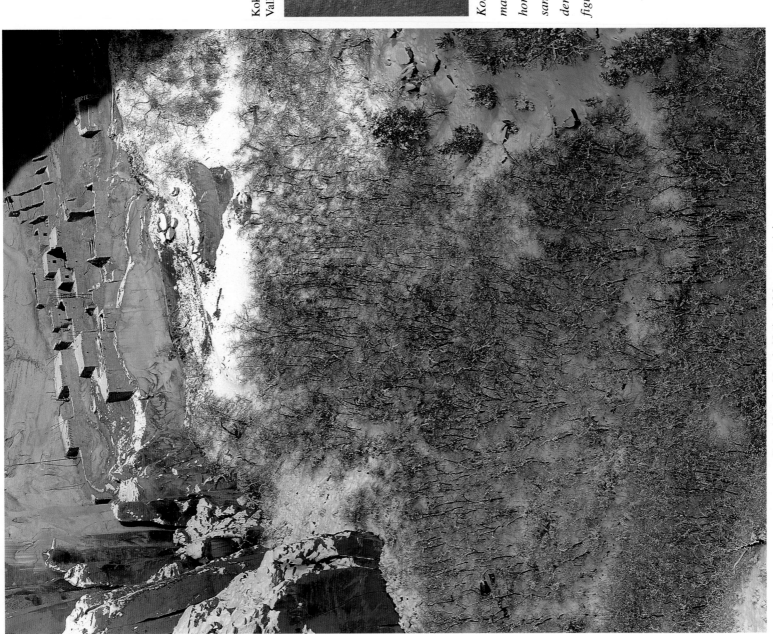

Betatakin ruin, Navajo National Monument, Arizona

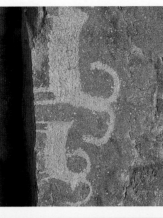

Fremont petroglyphs,
Desolation Canyon, Utah

makers, as they now fade from the
rocks that hold them. Though the
Anasazi disappeared, there is good
reason to think their descendants
live on in the pueblos of the
Southwest.

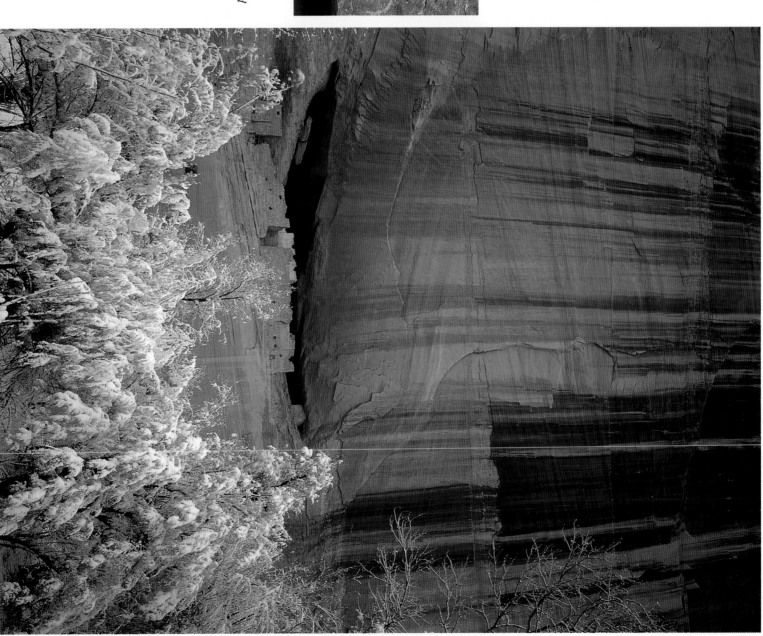

White House Ruin, Canyon de Chelly National Monument, Arizona

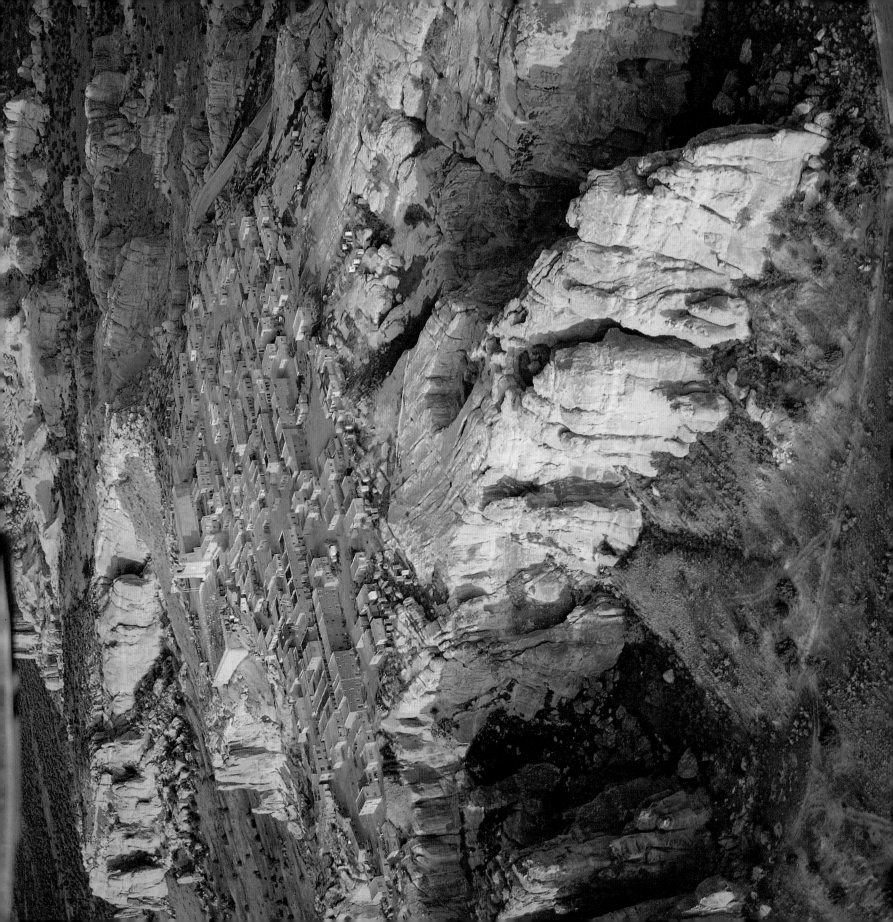

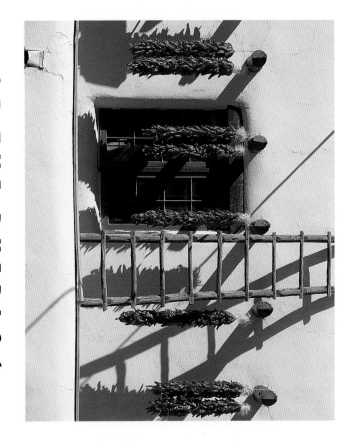

THE PEOPLE
OF THE PUEBLOS

Acoma Pueblo or Sky City, New Mexico
Above: Chili peppers, Taos Pueblo, New Mexico

THE PEOPLE OF THE PUEBLOS

When people came to this world, the Fourth World, they came because they wished to start anew. Many had forgotten the words of Spider Grandmother when she brought them to the Third World, which Tawa the Sun Spirit had created for them out of Endless Space. They had forgotten that Tawa had transformed them from beasts to humans, that Spider Grandmother had charged them to live in harmony and to forget evil. Some in their arrogance even came to believe that they had created themselves. Sorcerers worked their tricky magic, creating dissension. The kivas became gambling-houses; children wandered in the streets, dirty and unfed. Those who held to the right ways, who had not forgotten Tawa, were deeply troubled. They came together to decide what to do. Spider Grandmother came to them as they met, with a message from Tawa: "You must prepare to leave this place, to find another far from these evil ones." The people were further troubled at this. They did not know where to go.

Some of the elders had heard footsteps in the sky. They decided to investigate. They made a bird of clay and sang it to life, sending it flying up, up, up to the top of the sky to the sipapuni, the opening into the place above. Its ruler and only inhabitant, Masauwu, Spirit of Death and Owner of Fire, heard the message the bird carried and gave permission for those who so desired, to come live in his world.

The people made plans to depart. They did not know how they would reach the doorway in the sky. Spider Grandmother and her twin grandsons, the warrior gods, came to help. Chipmunk planted a bamboo stalk that the people sang to the top of the sky. As they climbed the long stalk and emerged through the sipapuni into the new world, Mockingbird assigned each a tribe and language, and sent each group in a different direction.

So came people to the Fourth World, according to Hopi legend. They came still charged with their original purpose: to forget evil and avoid injuring others, to live in harmony, to ponder the meaning of things. Each of their kivas, the gathering place for religious ceremonies and home of the Kachina Societies, still bears an indentation in the floor, a physical reminder of the original sipapuni. None now knows where that origin place is.

Perhaps it is in the depths of the Grand Canyon, perhaps in one of the low places between the fingers of Black Mesa, where the Hopi settled after their great wandering.

The Hopi live on a raised island surrounded by the Navajo reservation. The fingers of Black Mesa point south-southwest, toward Flagstaff and Winslow, toward Wupatki and Sunset Crater and Homol'ovi.

Moenkopi is at the far western edge of their land. Traveling west from Ganado on Highway 264, the first town is Keams Canyon, backed up against the mesa in a shaded vale. There must be water here; there are trees, and green grass, even in high summer. There is a sense of life suspended. No one is in view, no dogs bark, no people hustle by with purpose in the silent streets.

The Hopi live much closer together than the Navajo do. There seems to be more money here. Satellite dishes abound. More vehicles surround each family compound, and there are fewer house trailers. There's even a Hopi Civic Center between Kykotsmovi and Oraibi, across from the Mennonite mission. Newer houses are warm

yellow-brown boxes with square windows. Their outlines look surprisingly like the ruined rooms at Betatakin.

The Hopi are but one group of the many known collectively as the Pueblo people. Though distinct in language and origin, the Hopi, the Zuni, and the peoples of Acoma, Laguna, San Ildefonso, Santa Clara, Jemez, Taos, and the other pueblos of the Rio Grande share similar lives. All are experienced dry-land farmers, growing fine corn, squash, chilies, melons, and fruits in desert conditions. Most settled close together, in stone and adobe buildings atop the mesas and highlands overlooking their fields. These pueblos, so named by the Spanish, are the architectural descendants of the cliff dwellings.

Most of the Pueblo groups have managed to preserve their religious practices in the face of repression and cruelty, perpetrated first by Spanish missionaries, then through the concerted efforts of the Indian Bureau and the Anglo-Protestant church. Many now supplement their income by creating and selling art: fine overlay silver and gold jewelry by Hopi artisans; white and black pots from Acoma, decorated with geometric patterns that swell and shrink with the curve of the vessel's wall; black pots from Santa Clara, burnished until they have the sheen of metal; bracelets and rings from Zuni, inlaid with precisely cut semiprecious stones; incised, thick-walled red pots from Jemez; carved representations of Kachinas—the list grows as new styles and specialties are created.

The people of the Rio Grande pueblos welcomed the Spanish when they first arrived in the 1500s. In exchange for protection from Apache and Navajo raiders, the Pueblo peoples shared their desert-dwelling expertise, their agricultural bounty, and their religion. The missionaries repaid them by forcing them to become baptized, disrupting their ceremonies, and destroying their prayer sticks and altars. The Spanish were hard masters and greedy, taking what they wanted in the name of the Church. Many from the eastern pueblos moved west to the land of the Hopi, to avoid persecution by the Castillas. By the time the Spanish had been in the Southwest 140 years, the people of the pueblos had had enough. Represen-

tatives from each of the pueblos met in secret under the leadership of Popay, a Tewa from Santa Clara. Each was entrusted with a string with a number of knots in it. A knot was untied each day until the day came that the final knot was untied. On that day the people of the pueblos rose in rebellion, killed the priests and soldiers, and tore the churches down stone by stone. The Spanish who were not killed were driven back into Mexico.

When the Catholic Church returned to the Rio Grande pueblos after a number of years, native practices were not suppressed with the same vigor and the Spanish and natives settled into a period of harmony. There was much intermarriage, with many Pueblo families adopting Spanish surnames. For some time most people spoke both Spanish and the language of their village. A blend of Catholic and native religious ritual is still prevalent today. Some of the dances of the eastern pueblos are now held to coincide with the Church's high holidays. Many who fill the pews on Sunday are in the kivas the rest of the week.

Almost every Pueblo village has an open plaza, where the public part of traditional dances are held. Much of each ritual is open only to initiates, taking place in the kivas or otherwise out of sight. Each village and group has its own rituals, its own secret societies, though throughout all is the unifying link of personification of supernatural beings by humans: the Kachinas.

There is a rhythm and pace to the calendar of rituals that follows the patterns of nature, the weather, the phases of the moon. At winter solstice the great Shalako, messenger of the gods, comes to the Zuni. The Kachinas come from their homes in the sacred San Francisco Mountains to the west to spend time with the Hopi, instructing them and performing the ceremonies that ensure rain and abundance. In early summer, as the rainy season begins, the Kachinas return to their mountains, after the Niman, or home, dances are held in each village.

Each pueblo has its clowns, who have license to mock everything and everyone, and in so doing, to publicly admonish those who stray. At Zuni the Koyemsi, the Mudhead Kachinas, whose grotesque masks suggest the offspring of incestuous relations, are a vivid visual reminder to keep

to the right ways, the ways of the tribe.

In some ways the story of Old Oraibi, on Third Mesa, also reinforces that message. Containing the oldest continually occupied dwellings in the United States, Oraibi is going to pieces. It has never recovered from the exodus of its traditionalists, who departed in 1906 after a pushing contest against the Friendlies in the town square. The Friendlies wanted to comply with new government policies; the traditionalists, or Hostiles, did not. The Hostiles eventually formed a new village, Hotevilla, to the west of Oraibi. Hotevilla is now a center of traditional learning and a resource for the entire Hopi nation.

The people left in Oraibi destroyed their own kivas, their prayer sticks, and their masks. The dances and songs of their Kachina Societies were lost and never recovered. No initiations could be held—no one knew the rituals. Gradually those who stayed began to drift away; some to Hotevilla, some to form another village closer to the eastern edge of the mesa. Old Oraibi is still occupied, but it is a place of ghosts. While Hotevilla thrives, Oraibi returns to dust.

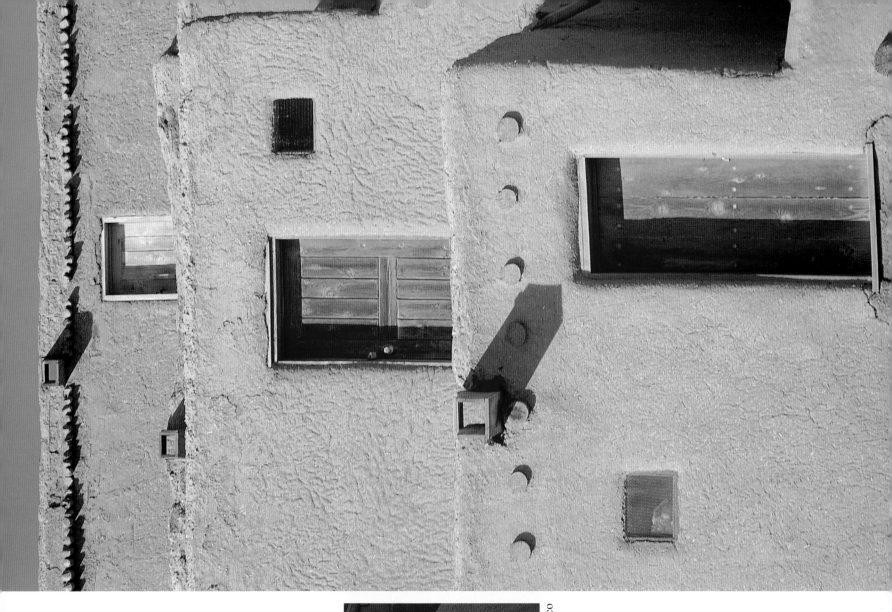

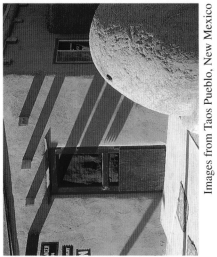

Images from Taos Pueblo, New Mexico

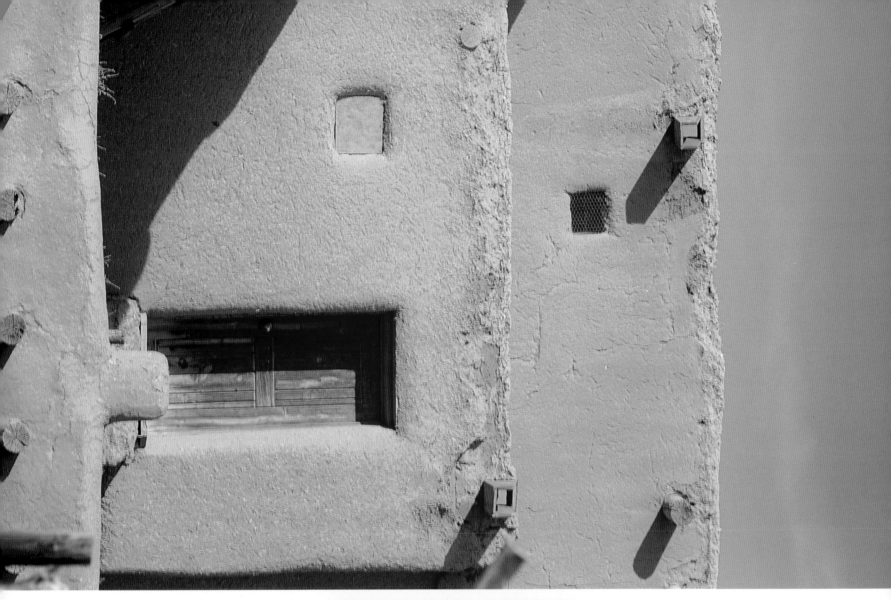

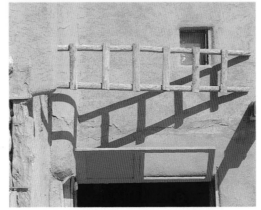

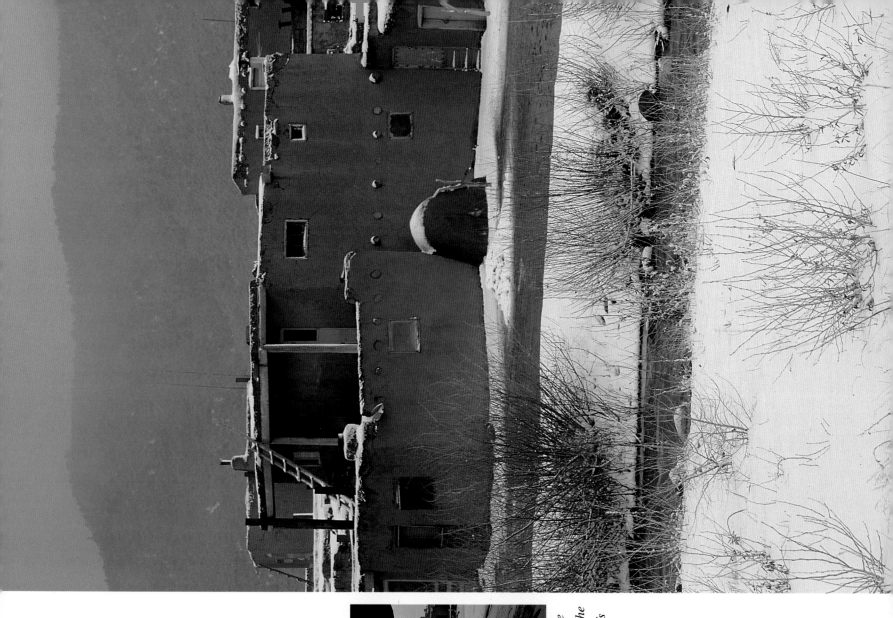

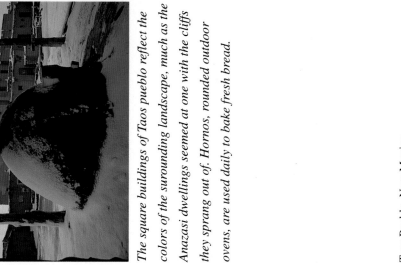

The square buildings of Taos pueblo reflect the colors of the surounding landscape, much as the Anazasi dwellings seemed at one with the cliffs they sprang out of. Hornos, rounded outdoor ovens, are used daily to bake fresh bread.

Taos Pueblo, New Mexico

42

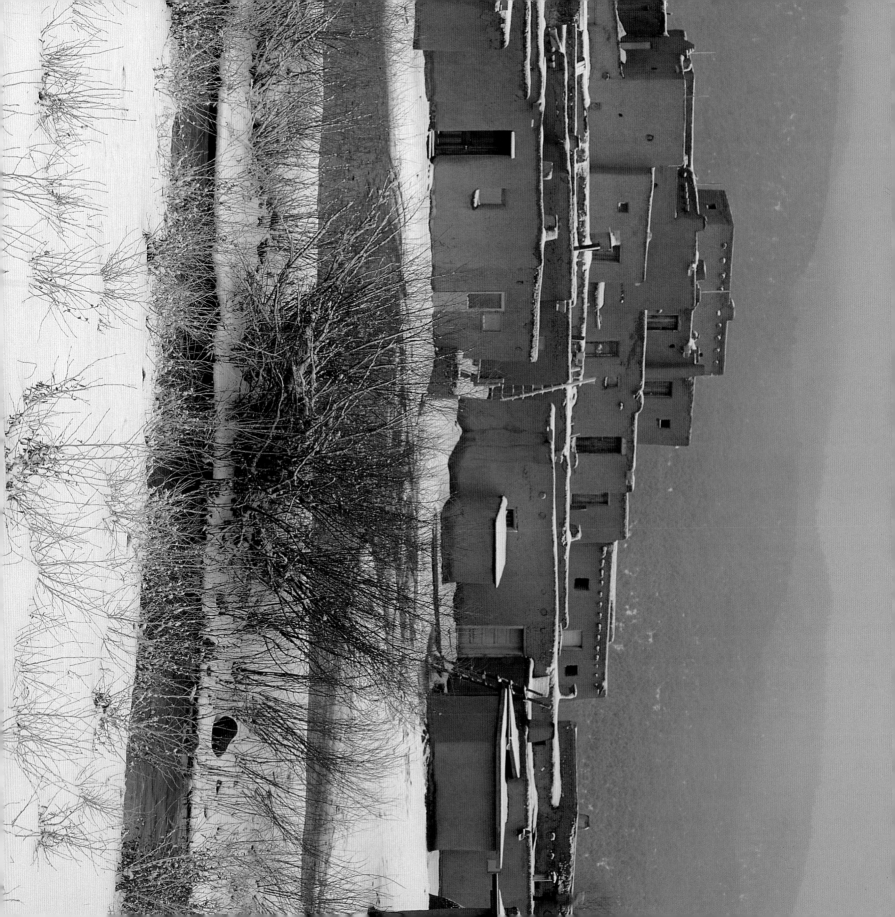

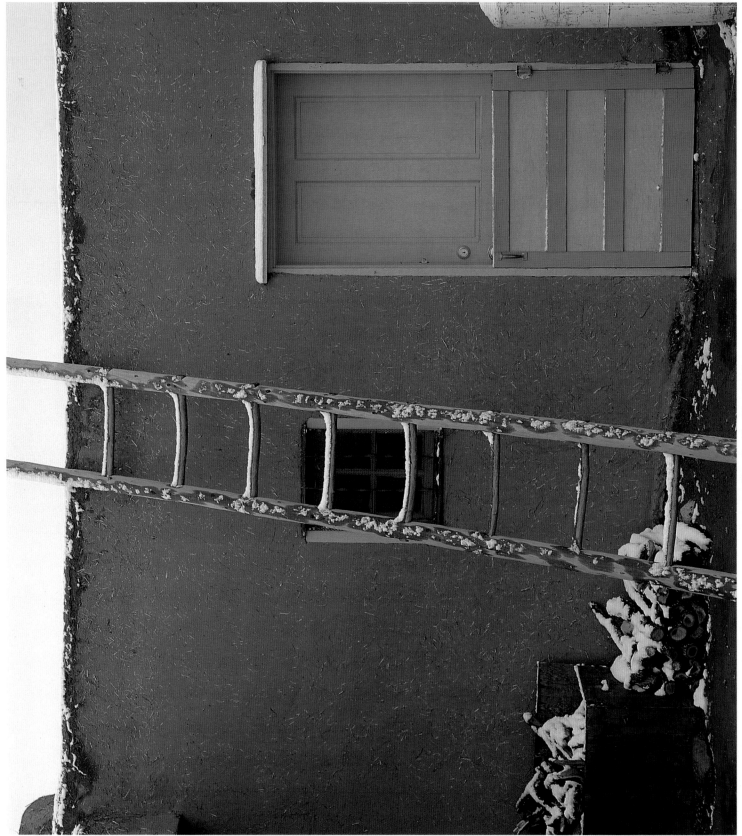

Taos Pueblo, New Mexico

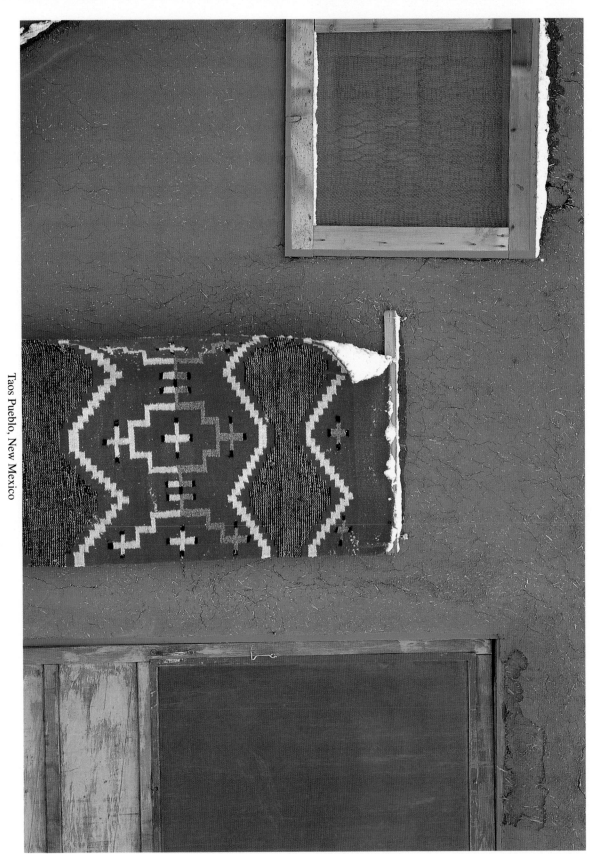

Taos Pueblo, New Mexico

Though weaving is not much practiced by the Puebloans today; they were
the original teachers of the Navajo. Hopi men are thought to have taught
the Navajo during the years they struggled together against the Spanish.

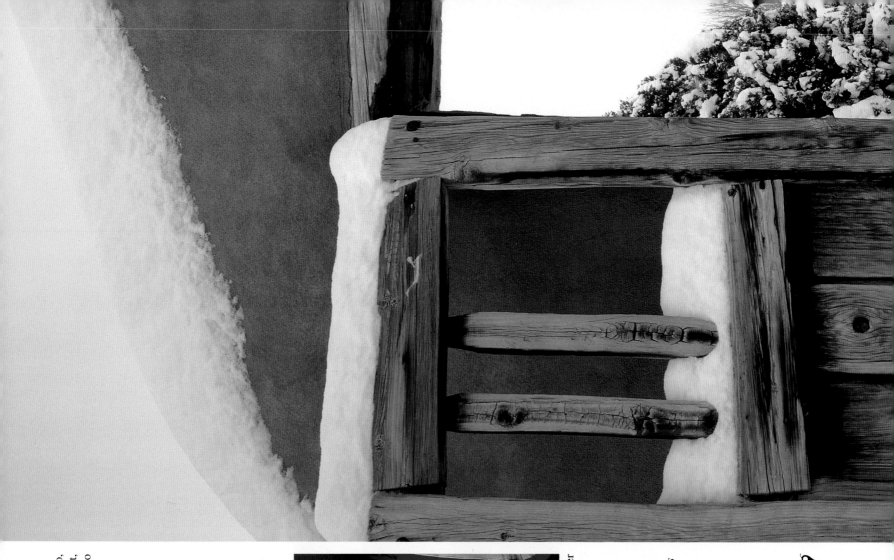

Sanctuario de Chimayo,
the Lourdes of the Southwest,
Chimayo, New Mexico

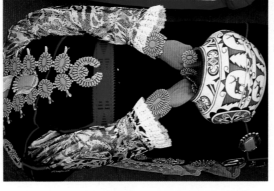

Zuni dancer

Catholicism, brought by the
Spanish in 1540, clashed with
native religious practice from the
outset. The early mission churches
were torn down during the rebellion of 1680. The new missions,
rebuilt after the Spanish returned,
are are now as much a part of
the Southwest as the pueblos
themselves.

46

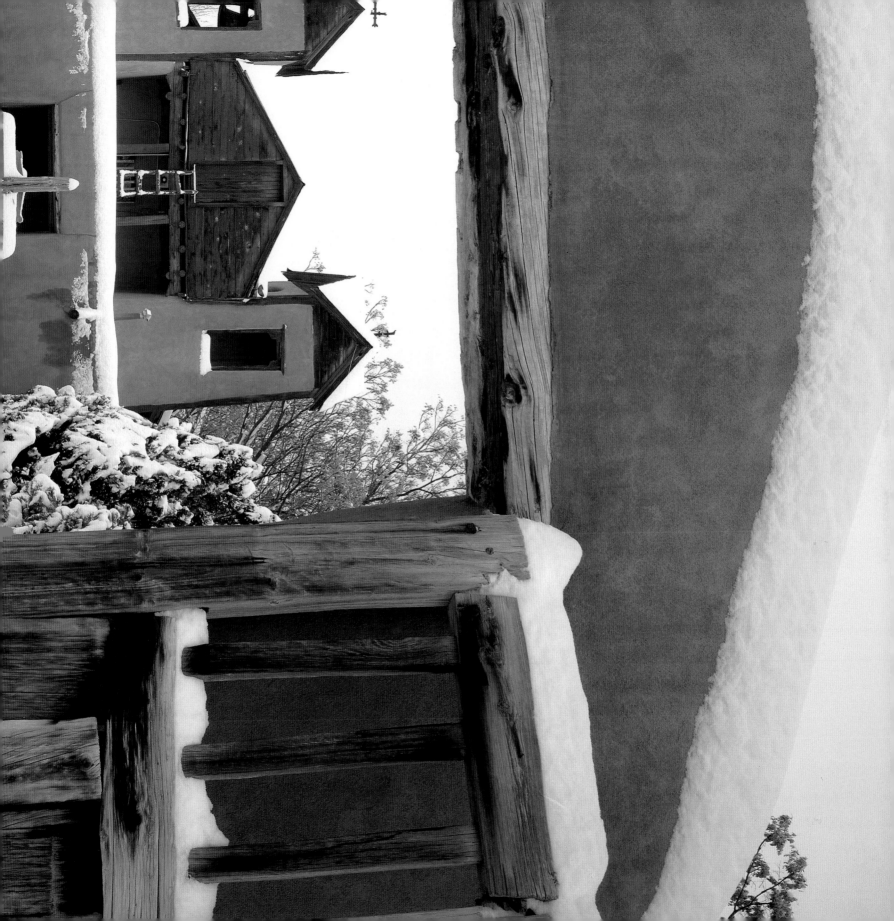

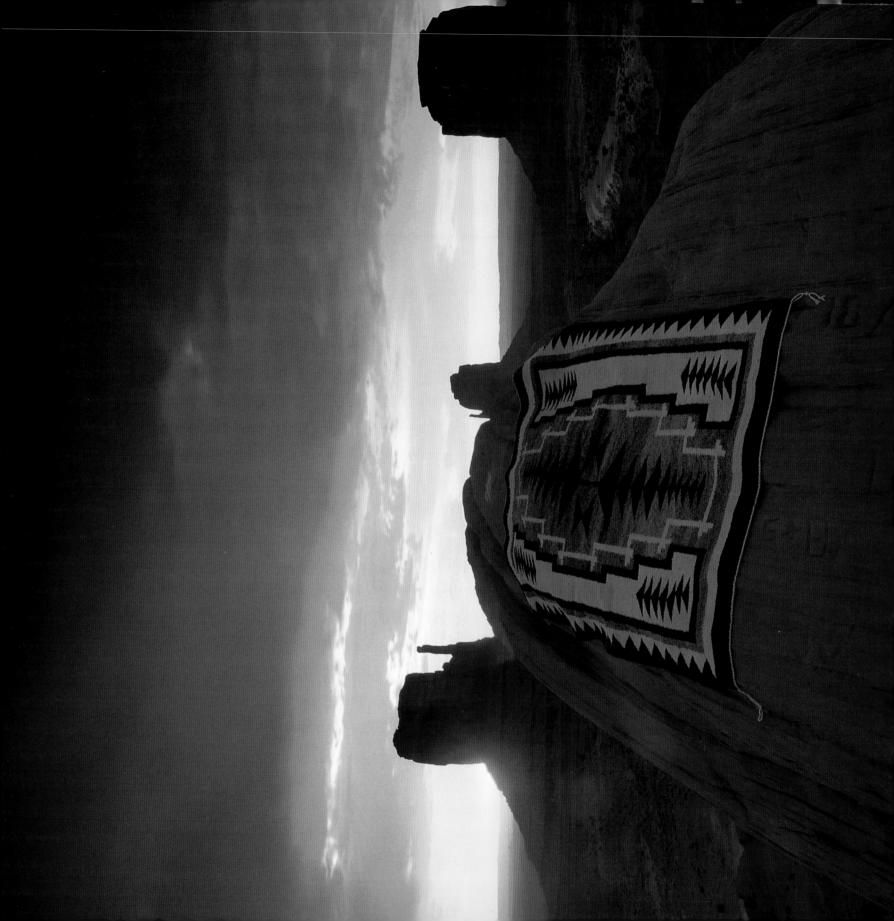

THE

NAVAJO

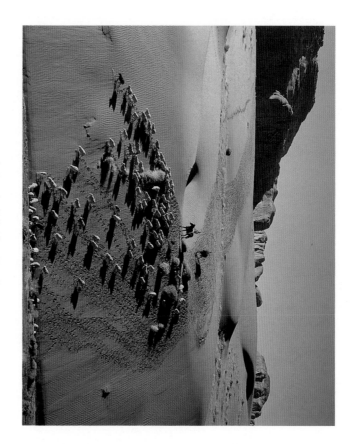

Modern rug in Two Gray Hills style, Monument Valley Tribal Park, Arizona
Above: Sheep and herders, Monument Valley Tribal Park, Arizona

THE NAVAJO

In the larger towns on the reservation, all paths cross at the laundromat or at Basha's, the main supermarket chain in Arizona, and the only one on the reservation. There are families in pickup trucks, six or seven crammed in a king cab: Mom, Dad, and little girls in the front, three boys in the jump seats. For some this is a 30- or 40-mile round trip. They bring coolers so their perishables won't spoil in the desert heat on the trip home. Horses and cows wander the streets, occasionally stopping traffic. Packs of barely domesticated dogs pass by, scrapping and sniffing and checking for things to eat. An old woman in traditional Navajo garb—black shoes, white anklets, flowing flowered skirt with gray background, purple velvet shirt, huge turquoise bracelet, coral and turquoise watchband—hurries from her pickup truck, supported by her cane.

The larger towns are separated by miles of open land. Sparsely scattered hogans, some of logs, some of lumber and tarpaper, are tenuously connected by dirt roads to the main highways. Sometimes, where the map indicates a town, there is nothing but a cluster of trailers or a lone chapter house. Rock is always nearby, sometimes rounded and smooth, sometimes sharp and tearing. And above all, miles of sky, thin blue air, endless vistas of open space. One must learn to adapt to loneliness early here.

The Navajo, or Dineh, as they call themselves, have always been an adaptable and practical people, borrowing from many traditions and transforming them into something uniquely their own. Athapascan-speaking latecomers to the Southwest, they and the Apache migrated from the north, possibly in the late fifteenth century. They adapted quickly to a life of herding and raiding, using their horses to harass the more settled Pueblo peoples by stealing livestock and food. They learned metal-working from the Spanish and weaving from the Pueblo peoples who, ironically, joined with them during the years of heaviest

Spanish oppression. They refined their weaving skills by adopting the tapestry style favored by the Spanish, at first producing simple clothing for themselves and blankets and other weavings for trade.

Subdued finally by the brutality of Kit Carson's campaign against them in the 1860s, most Navajo were banded together and marched to Bosque Redondo, on the Pecos River in New Mexico, some 300 miles from their homeland between the four sacred mountains. Finally returned to their lands after six years, they became prosperous by raising sheep, goats, and cattle. Prosperity led to greater numbers—more people and larger herds of livestock taxing the resources of their desert land. The government indiscriminately carried out forced herd reduction in the 1930s, a devastating and inexplicable practice, especially to those Navajo families who remembered the privation of the early reservation years. Navajo religious beliefs may have been influ-

enced by the Pueblo peoples, but the practice was uniquely adapted and transformed. The Navajo do not believe in an afterlife. Understandably, then, there is an emphasis on living fully while here. Religion is not kept on the shelf for special days, but is part of daily routine. For example, all traditional hogans face east, so that the rising sun can be greeted in song.

It is of primary importance to the Navajo to live a balanced and harmonious life, to "walk in beauty." Life lived out of balance can bring problems not only for the individual but for the group. Most of the great Navajo ceremonies, called *sings*, are carried out to restore harmony and balance to the person the sing is held for, but benefits are enjoyed by all. This need for harmony, for balance and beauty, carries over into all work and especially into the weaving and silversmithing that define Navajo craft.

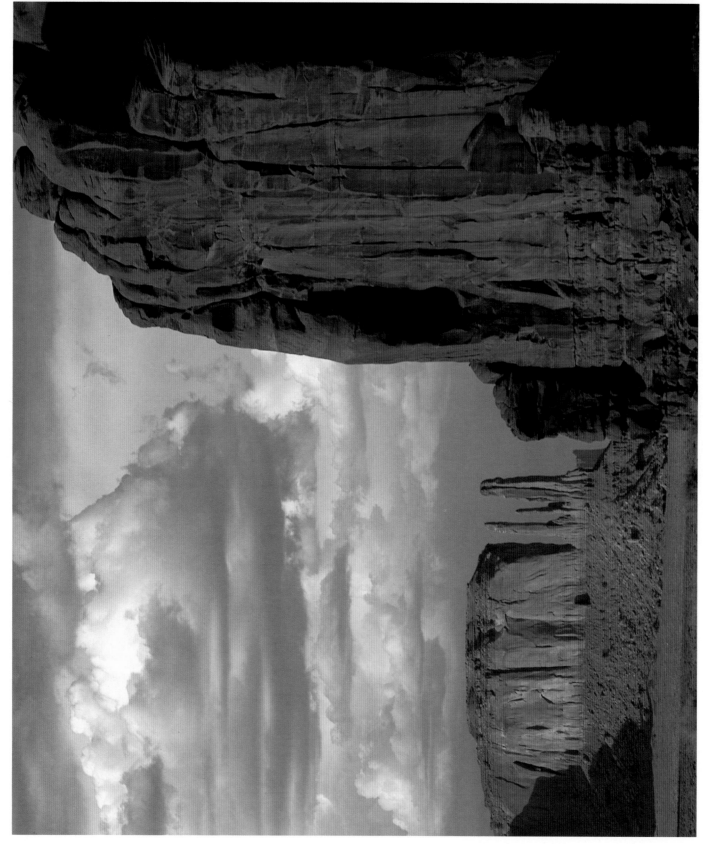

Three Sisters, Monument Valley Tribal Park, Arizona

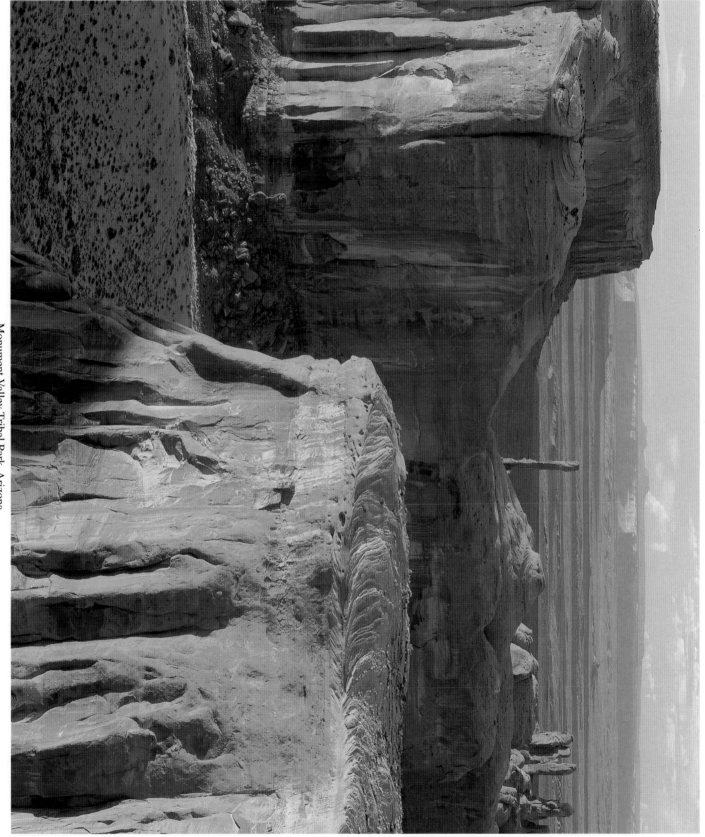

Monument Valley Tribal Park, Arizona

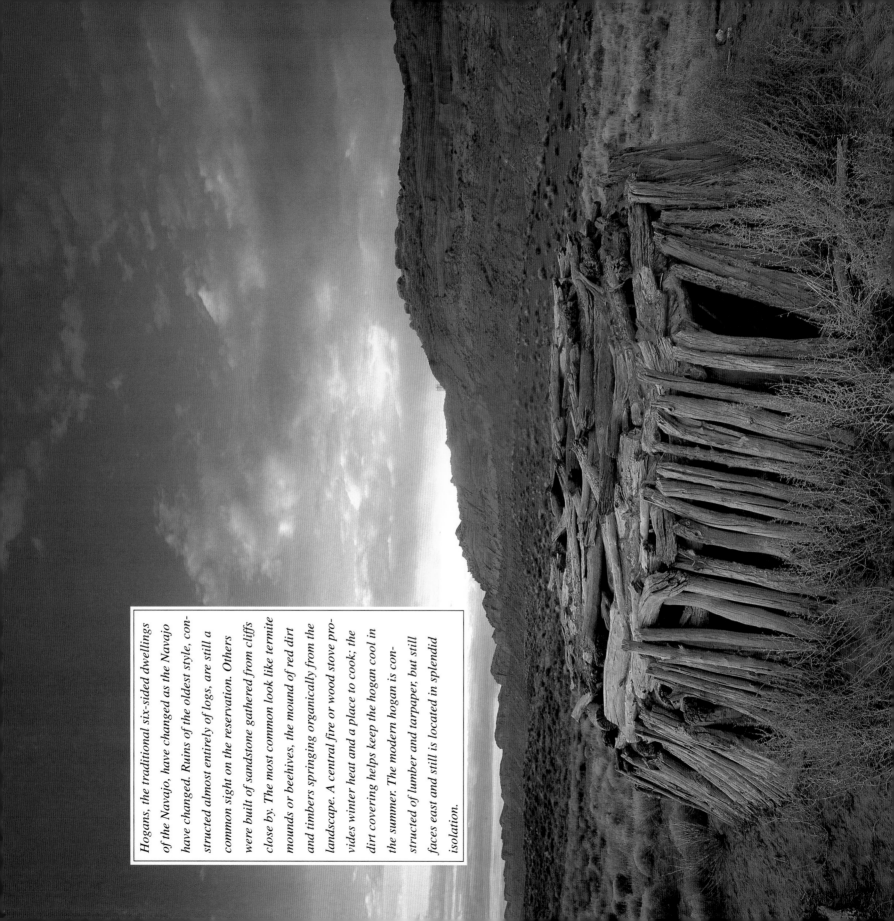

Hogans, the traditional six-sided dwellings of the Navajo, have changed as the Navajo have changed. Ruins of the oldest style, constructed almost entirely of logs, are still a common sight on the reservation. Others were built of sandstone gathered from cliffs close by. The most common look like termite mounds or beehives, the mound of red dirt and timbers springing organically from the landscape. A central fire or wood stove provides winter heat and a place to cook; the dirt covering helps keep the hogan cool in the summer. The modern hogan is constructed of lumber and tarpaper, but still faces east and still is located in splendid isolation.

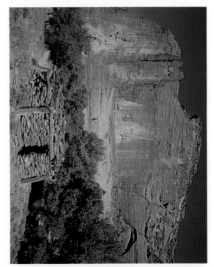

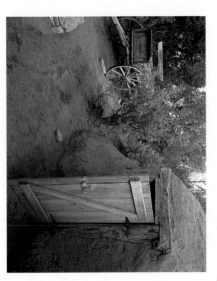

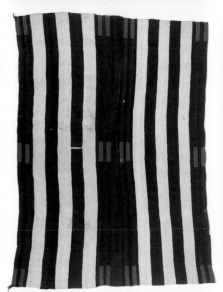

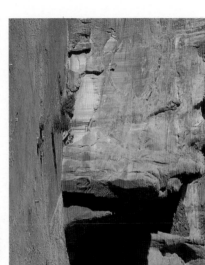

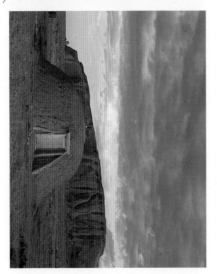

Phase II chief blanket, 1860, courtesy San Diego Museum of Man

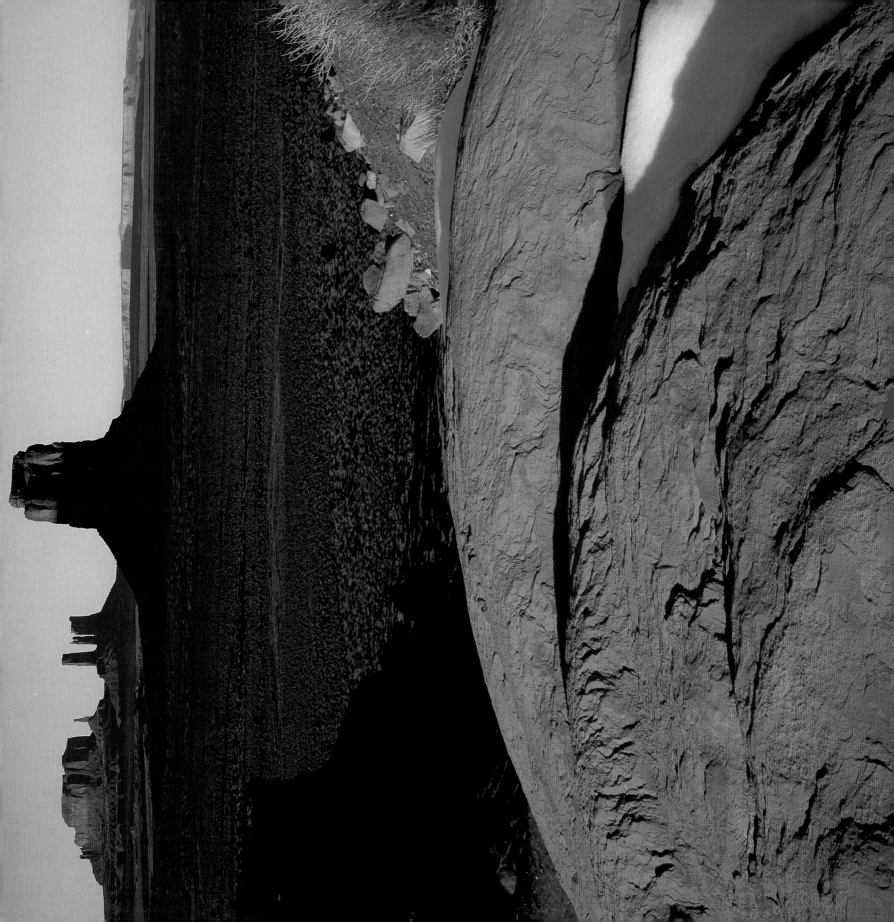

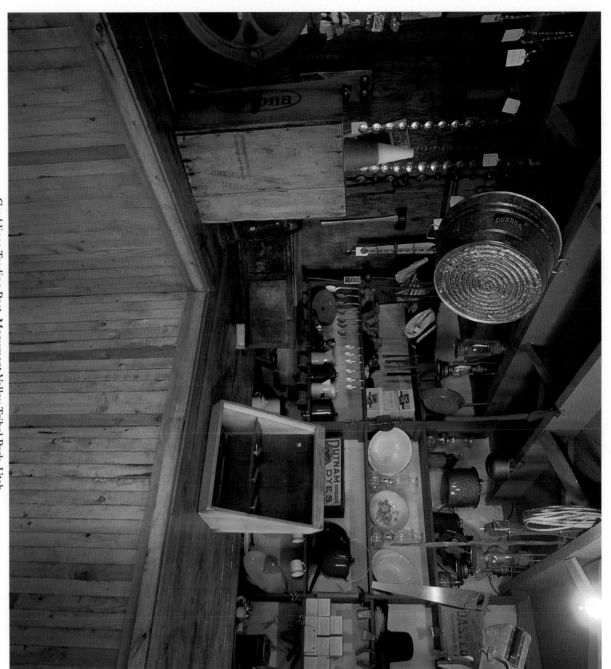

Gouldings Trading Post, Monument Valley Tribal Park, Utah

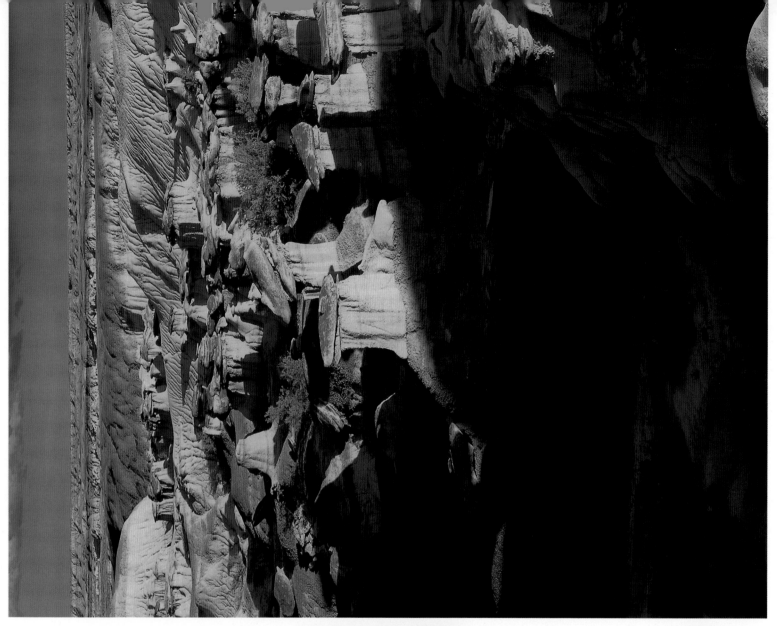

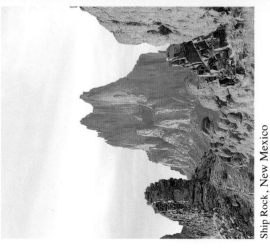

Ship Rock, New Mexico

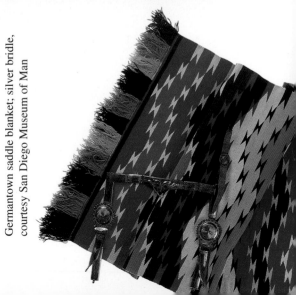

Germantown saddle blanket; silver bridle,
courtesy San Diego Museum of Man

58

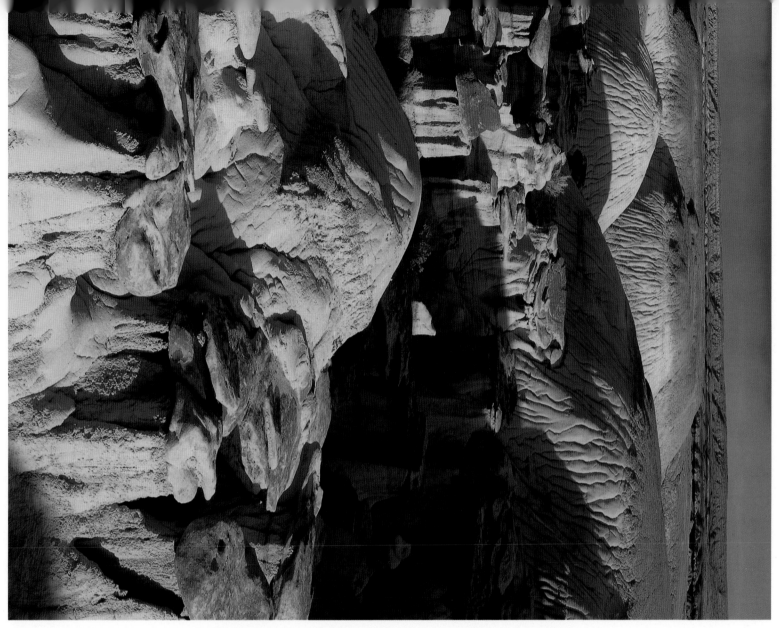

Strange land forms define
the Southwest as surely as
they dominate it, from lumpy
gray hoodoos to the tower-
ing blackness of Ship Rock.
Navajoland itself is defined
by four sacred mountains—
Doko'ooslííd (San Fran-
cisco Peak) to the west,
Dibeítsaa (Mount Hesperus)
to the north, Sisnaajiní
(Sierra Blanca) to the east,
and Tsoodził (Mount Taylor)
to the south—but Ship Rock
dominates its eastern skies.
This hard basaltic neck,
casting long shadows over
the land, is the only remnant
of a volcano, long ago
eroded away.

Hoodoos, Ah-Shi-Sie-Pah, New Mexico

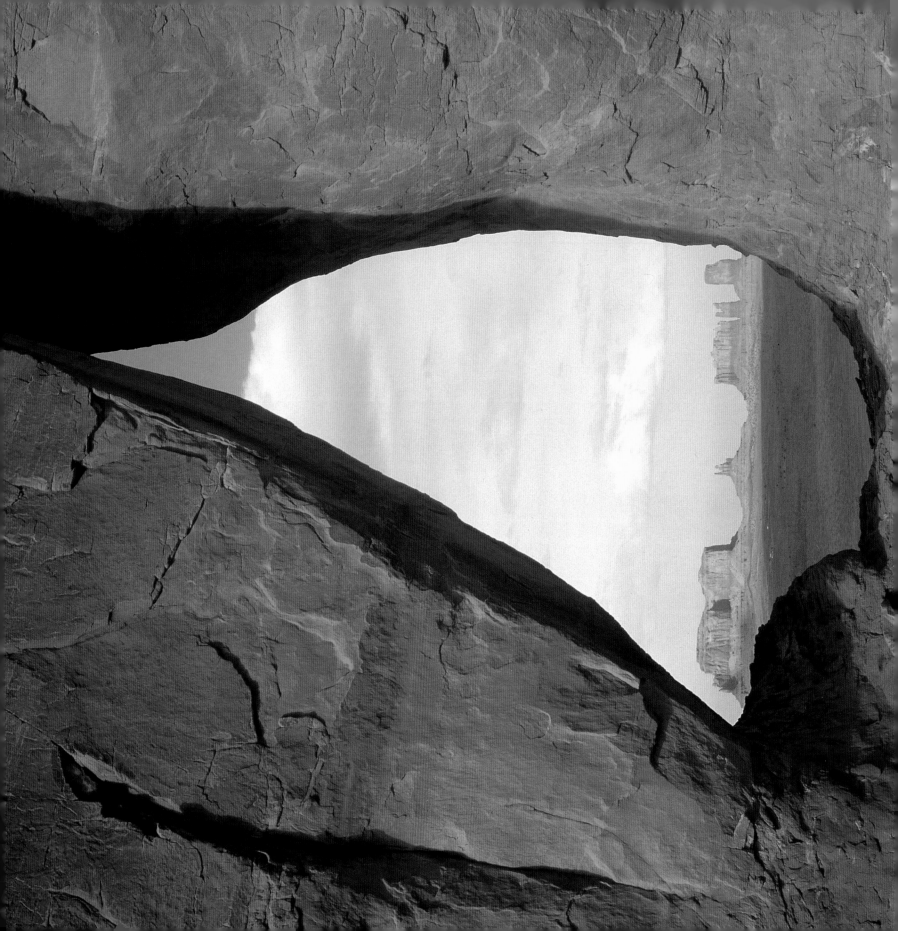

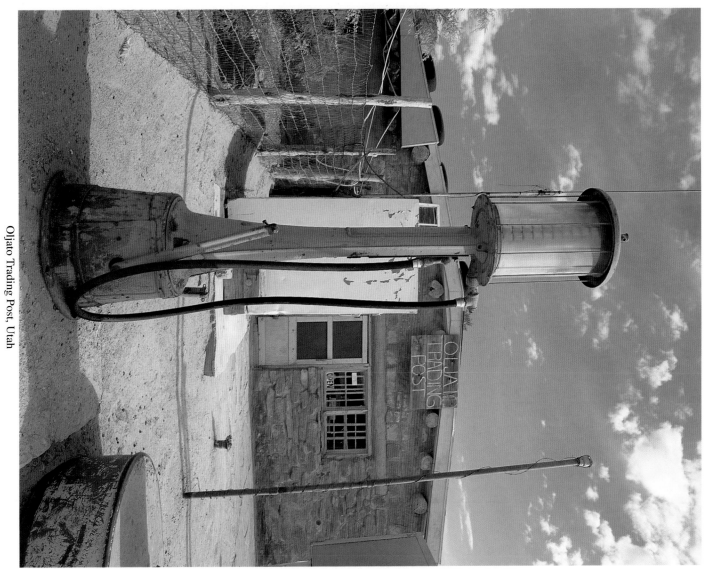

Oljato Trading Post, Utah

CAMERON TRADING POST

Cameron Trading Post sits on the Little Colorado River at the far southwest corner of the reservation, just after the junction of Arizona State Highways 89 and 64. Turn west to the Grand Canyon, past the scattered hogans and open-air stands of the Navajo Nation. The road north takes you to Tuba City, to Kayenta, to Monument Valley, to Mexican Hat and the Utah border. There is not much to see on the highway between Flagstaff and Cameron—miles and miles of grass and desolation, broken up occasionally by a herd of grazing sheep or a dirt road to the left or right. There's not much in Cameron except the trading post, six house trailers, a gas station, and a Navajo-run arts and crafts cooperative.

Within the trading post compound itself are a feed store, a motel, a gallery of antiquities, a large gift shop, a cafeteria and restaurant, and a general store. All are built of pink-brown sandstone cut

from the cliffs of the gorge behind the compound. Cameron has been a tourist destination since the time of the first trader in 1916. Old photographs on the gift shop wall show carloads of tourists in Model Ts and Model As having their pictures taken next to the suspension bridge over the Little Colorado. Present-day diesel buses idle in the parking lot next to dusty rental cars and the beat-up trucks of the locals.

The dining room at Cameron has a high, unpainted, stamped-tin ceiling. Old pharmacy cabinets now serve as backdrops to intricate weavings of gray, red, black, and cream. A huge fireplace, flanked by two windows that look out into the gorge, dominates the west wall. The fireplace and the central support beam of the room are of the same brown stone as the exterior. The mantel and hearth of the fireplace are crammed with pottery and large Kachina figures, two of which stand on stone shelves jutting out above. Large tables are shoved together to accommodate hungry tour bus groups. The adventurous order Navajo tacos and Indian fry bread.

The gift shop has something for every pocketbook. Cheap, mass-produced "Indian" trinkets compete with gracefully rounded, hand-made Pueblo pots of tan and black; base-metal "authentic" charms drape over case after case of inlaid silver and stone rings; Arizona T-shirts vie for space with tiny, delicate, incised pots no bigger than a quail egg. The gallery across the parking lot is closed in preparation for its annual auction in October, but a friendly clerk unlocks it for viewing. Inside its cool, dark interior are burnished black pots and old rugs, massive silver bracelets, heavy squash-blossom necklaces inset with coral and turquoise, a set of Spanish spurs.

In the general store bolts of bright velvet—

royal blue, forest green, purple, red, and brown—hang from the ceiling next to lanterns and pale-green plastic lassos. Every inch of space is used. Hanks of hand-spun wool hang over the front register and the display case full of beads; saddle blankets are draped over the 50-pound cloth bags of flour. Axes, nursing bottles for livestock, and chain saws share shelves with canned goods, spices, and Shake-n-Bake. The produce department is a set of six wooden bins containing apples, onions, and potatoes—hardy items with a long shelf life. More exotic produce is available in the cold case next to the butcher's counter. Salt licks are $6.25 here, rolled milo $9.75, scratch feed $9.75, horseshoes $2.49 per pound. A new white gas range waits to be bought near the back entrance. This is the closest thing to a grocery store for 30 miles in any direction, the closest thing to a department store for 100 miles.

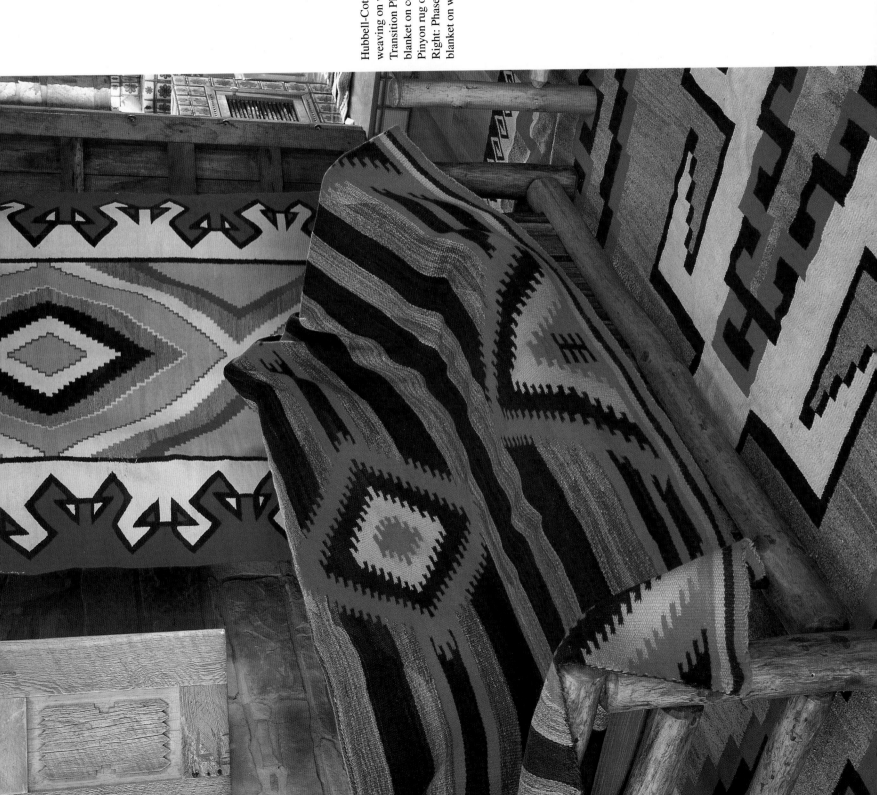

Hubbell-Cotton-Moore
weaving on wall, 1900;
Transition Phase wearing
blanket on couch, 1890;
Pinyon rug on floor, 1960
Right: Phase III chief
blanket on wall.

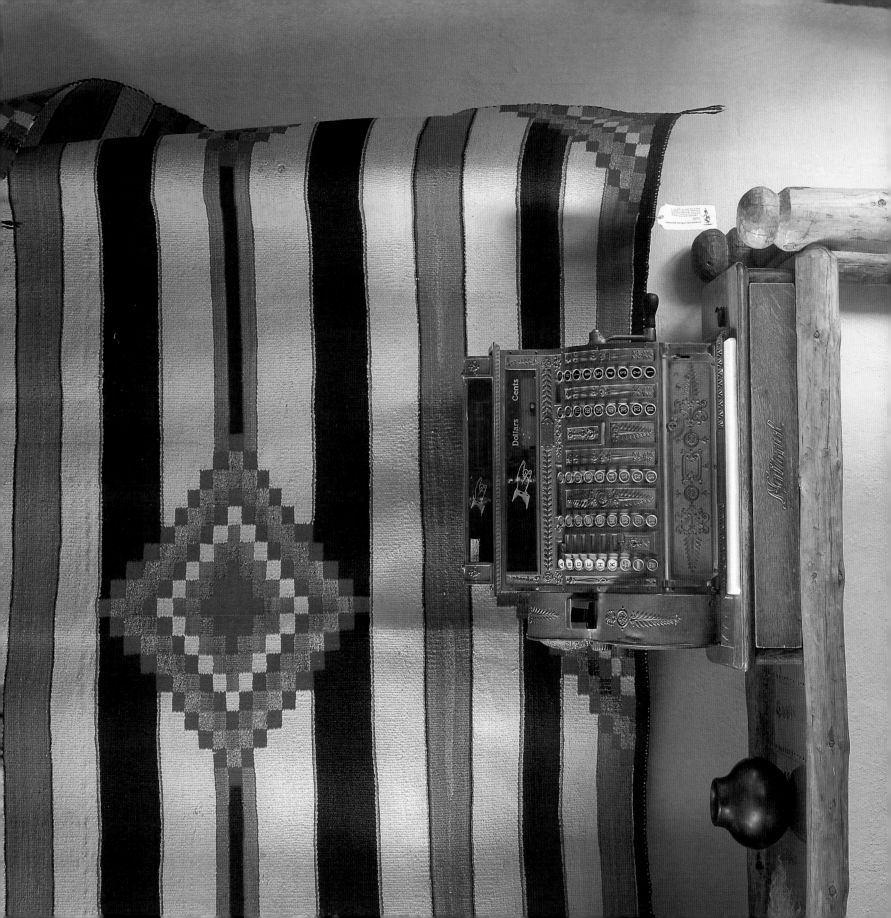

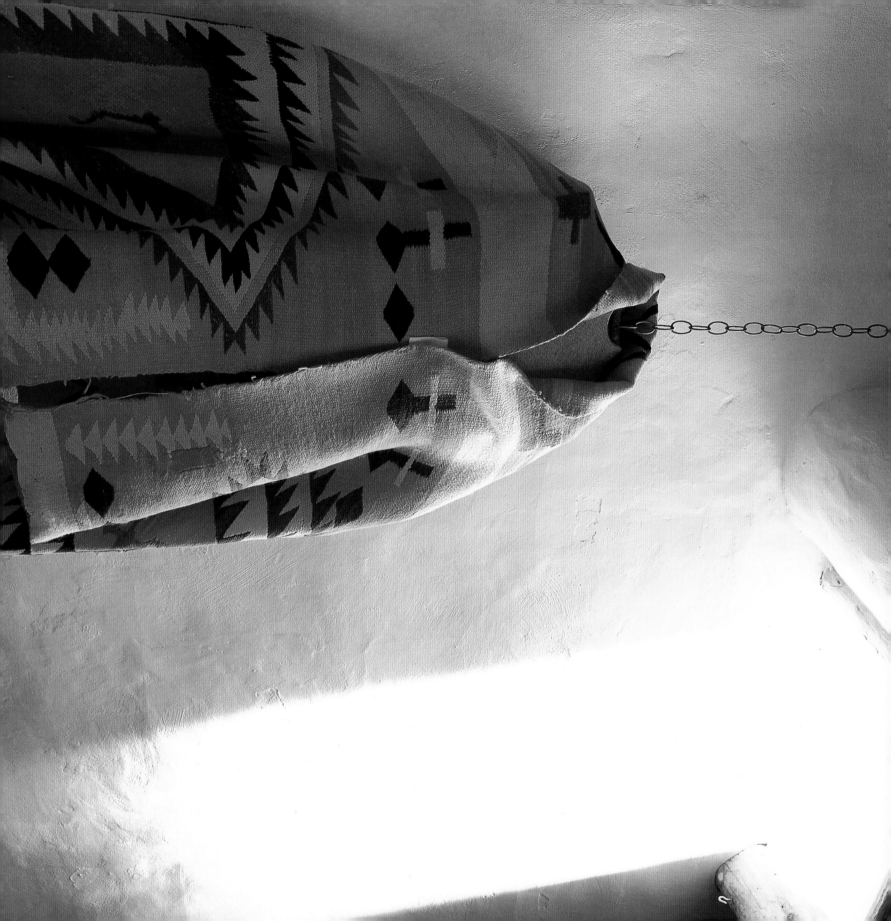

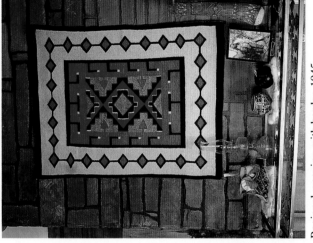

Regional weaving with border, 1945

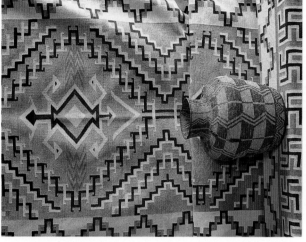

Two Gray Hills rug; Apache olla

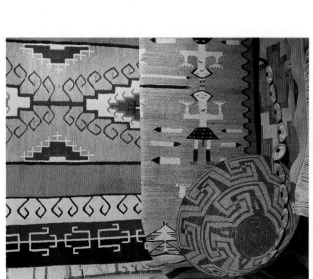

Teec Nos Pos rug on wall; Pima basket;
Ganado rug, 1940 Below: Silver concho belt

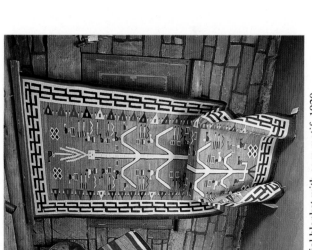

Pictorial blanket with corn motif, 1920

Transition
Phase wearing
blanket, 1880

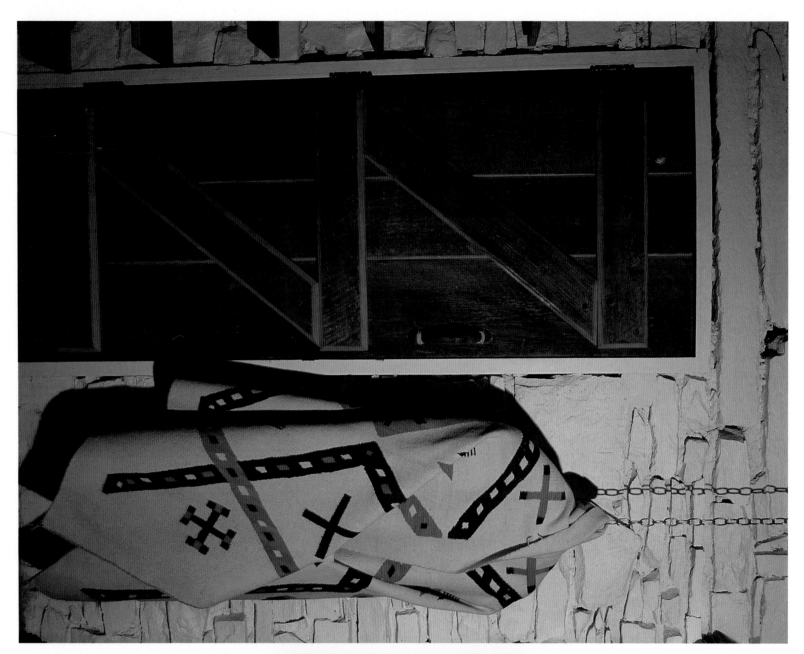

Transition Phase wearing blanket

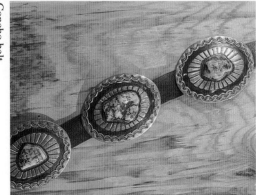

Concho belt

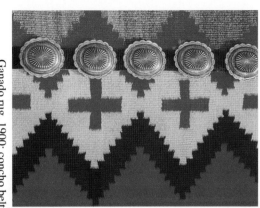

Ganado rug, 1900; concho belt

Phase III chief blanket

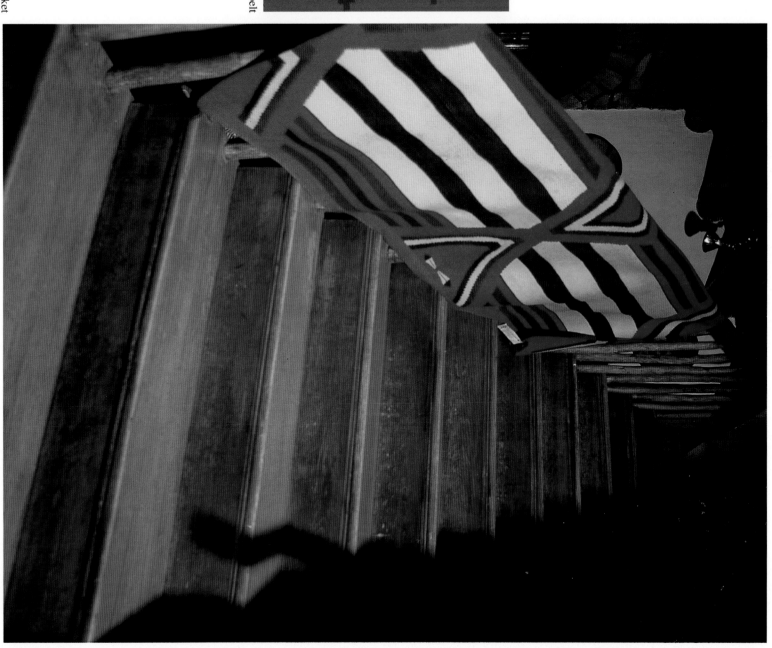

HUBBELL TRADING POST

Across Black Mesa to the east and south of Canyon de Chelly, on the Pueblo Colorado Wash, is the Hubbell Trading Post National Historic Site. If Cameron is the bustling present, Hubbell is the preserved and authentic past. The home of Lorenzo Hubbell and his family from the 1870s until the 1960s, the Hubbell Trading Post was purchased by the National Park Service in 1967 and preserved as a National Historic Site. It is still an active trading post, although pawn is no longer accepted, and the tin scrip Hubbell used to hand out to his workers and customers was called in long ago.

The trading post is a long, low building of brown sandstone, much darker than the stone used at Cameron. To the left as you face the buildings is the stable, now filled with old wagons. The front door of the old general store is flanked by two wagon wheels. The original display cases are still in use, and baskets hung on the pine ceiling beams in the rest of the trading post by the Hubbell daughters are still there. The old floorboards are warped, and shiny from years of being

swept. Most of the goods in the bull pen are behind the counter on shelves or laid out in display cases: rakes, work gloves, wool carders, yard goods, Kachinas, salad dressing, soup, picnic snacks, socks. Old horse harnesses hang from the ceiling.

A door to the right leads to the next room, dark and crowded with books and curios. Two large oil paintings, probably the gifts of artists who stayed with the Hubbells, hang over the jewelry counter. One is of a Kachina dance, the other of a Navajo family at home in their hogan. Perhaps the pawn rack was in this room, aglitter with heavy silver and turquoise bracelets and necklaces, and worn leather belts encircled by large stamped conchos. Navajo wealth is still often amassed in jewelry, easily carried on the body and, in earlier days, easily pawned for coffee beans and flour to tide the family over until the sheep were shorn or the pine nuts were ready to harvest.

The rug room is still here, off to the right. Each trading post has a rug room: each has its own character. Cameron's rug room is a fenced-off section at the back of the store, filled with small, brightly colored, mostly pictorial weavings. At Tuba City the rugs, mainly in rich, dark tones, hang on racks around the circumference of the eight-sided main building. The rug room at Hubbell is legendary. Hundreds of weavings lie spread out on the floor, or draped over racks in front of the bookcases, still filled with Hubbell's books, that line one wall. Above the bookcases are several dozen small watercolors of rug patterns. Each rug carries a tag certifying its origin, naming its pattern, identifying its weaver. Some names are as evocative as the rugs themselves: Burntwater, Storm, Crystal, New Lands, Tree of Life. Others more closely anchor the rug to the place of its design's origin: Klagetoh, Chinle, Teec Nos Pos, Two Gray Hills. The rich reds of the Ganados call the eye to them immediately; other, subtler colors and patterns are discovered and appreciated later. A line of tall, slender figures holding pine boughs or rattles fills the center of the Yei rugs. The Yei are the Navajo holy ones, supernatural beings who control the universe and who may be prevailed upon to bring harmony. These and the sandpainting rugs are controversial, since they present mysteries of the Navajo religion perhaps best not shared with outsiders.

Many of the trading posts are associated with a particular style of rug, promoted by and sometimes designed by the trader, based on what the trader thought the market back East would be interested in. Hubbell and John Moore at Crystal had catalogs printed for direct mail order. In many ways the traders were responsible for the continued growth of the rug market, both in providing a sales outlet for weavings and in promoting high standards of quality. Both the McSparrons at Chinle and the Lippincotts at Wide Ruins encouraged the use of natural dyes made from native plants.

The Hubbell house, completed in 1902, is behind the trading post. The living room and bedroom floors are covered with gigantic weavings, replicas of the rugs that were once here. Each was a one-year project for two weavers working together. Baskets hang from the rafters here also.

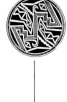

Drawings and portraits hang almost floor to ceiling, more gifts from guests of the Hubbell household. In contrast to the living room's Southwest decor, the dining room has an elaborately carved table, chairs, and sideboard, shipped from Europe at great expense. Hubbell lived here alone for long stretches of time, his wife preferring the charms of Albuquerque to the wilds of Ganado.

Once traders like Hubbell were the Navajos' main contact with the world outside the reservation, bringing them goods as well as helping them deal with Belecana, or white, ways. The trader would have written letters to government officials; sponsored contests; provided first aid; lent money on personal goods; purchased rugs, wool and sheep; buried the dead. Now the trader is a hazy memory. From a peak in 1943 of 95 trading posts on the reservation and 50 or more right outside its borders, there are now a handful of active posts.

Many of the old posts are now no more than souvenir stands. Others burned down and were never rebuilt. Traders at isolated posts could

stand their solitude only up to a point. Then they sold out or closed, never to return. The small communities have convenience stores; the larger ones have Basha's. In some ways, Basha's has taken over the functions of the trading post general store, offering chicken feed and salt licks alongside its in-store bakery and deli goods. The Navajo themselves are filling the trader's other roles. Elected tribal councils run the reservation, and tribal police help keep law and order. Some weavers are dealing directly with eager collectors rather than working through traders. Others are members of Navajo-run co-ops. Where once the Navajos' experience of the off-reservation world was filtered through the trader, cable TV and satellite dishes bring a superfluity of new ideas and influences directly into the hogan. Improved roads have meant increased mobility and greater access to off-reservation services and goods. Perhaps a mixed blessing for the people of the Blessing Way.

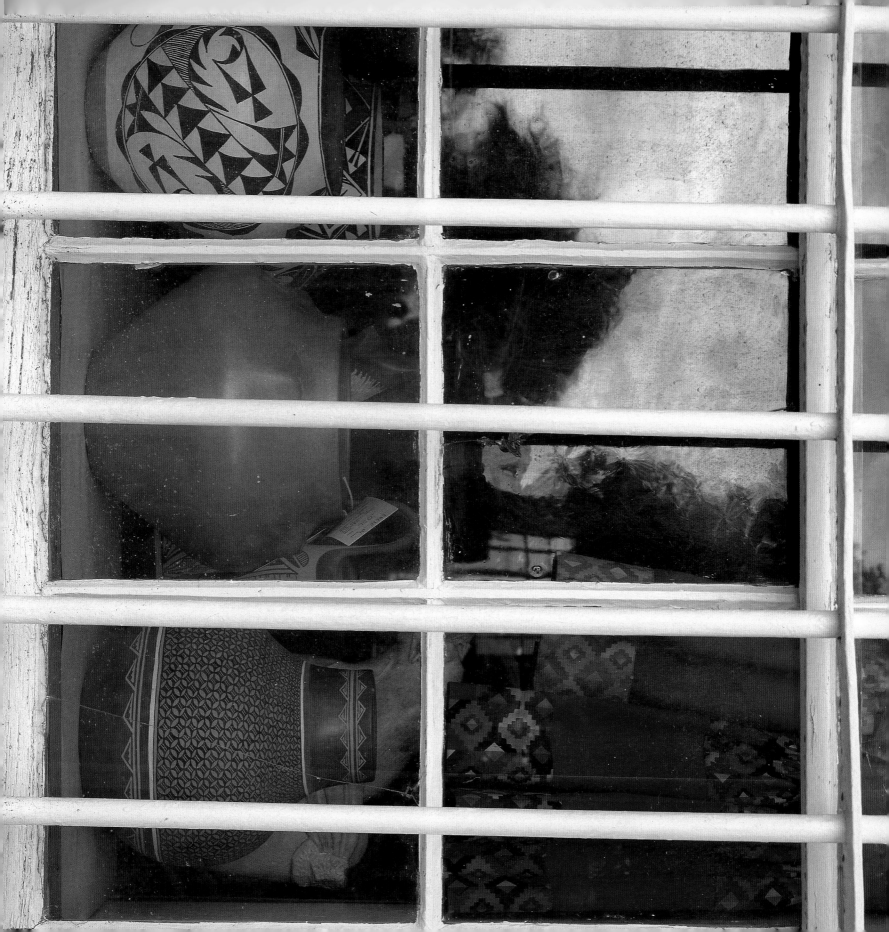

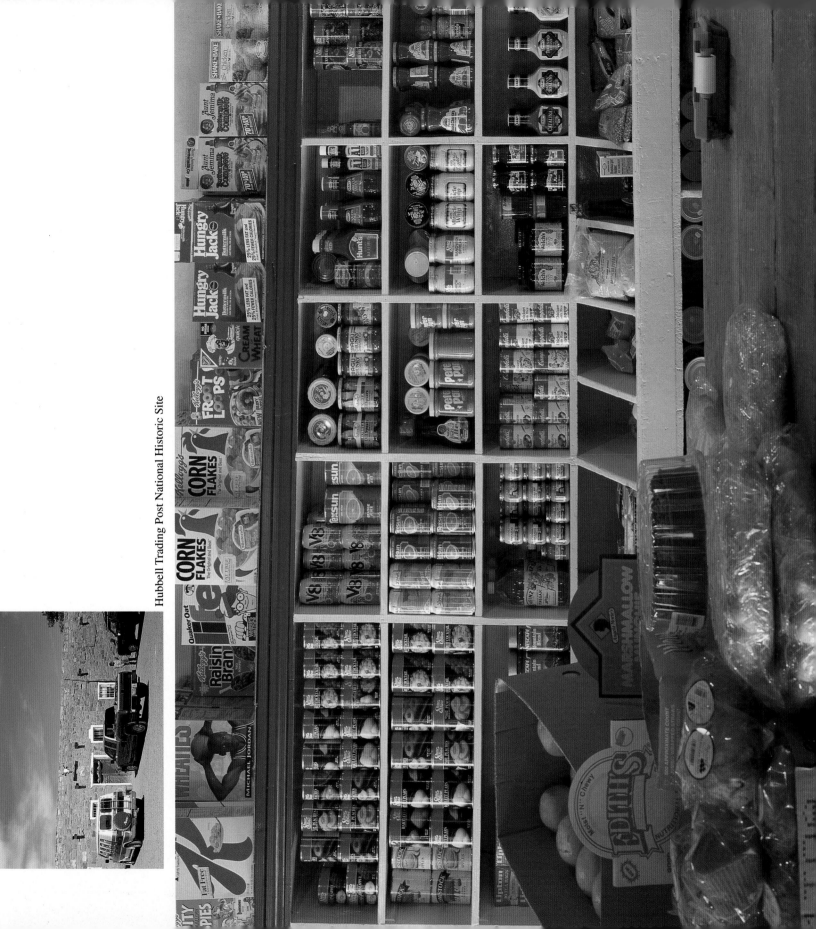

Hubbell Trading Post National Historic Site

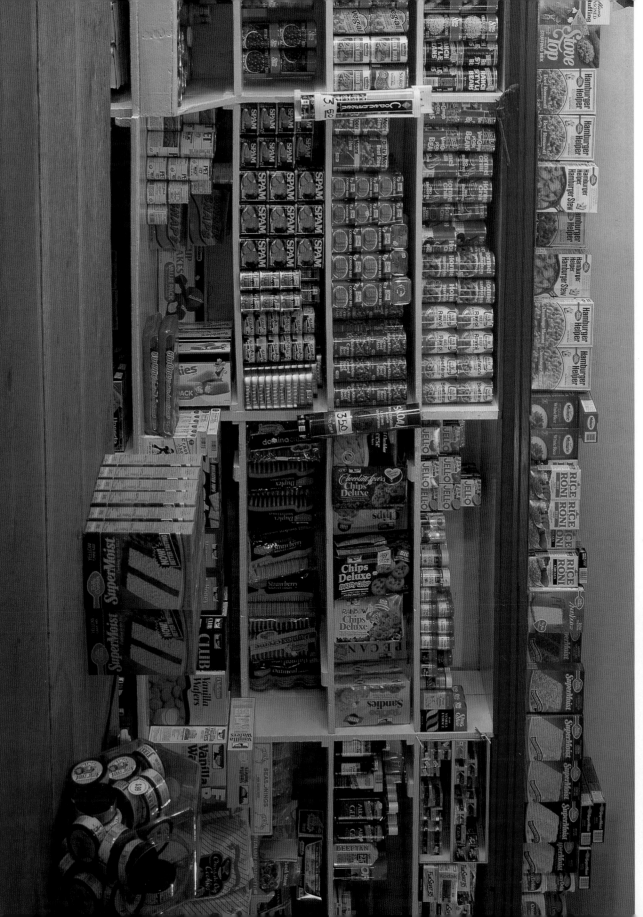

General store

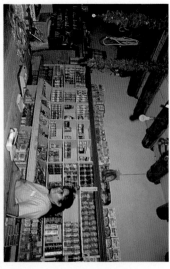

Fine silver conchos hanging from leather belts echo the rounded shapes of the coiled Hopi and Apache baskets hanging from Hubbell's rafters. Their rich variety of design is made up of combinations of simple motifs stamped, punched, and carved into the metal. Conchos and buttons, necklaces and beads, were all hammered out of coin silver by the first silversmiths.

Pillow cover, 1920, courtesy San Diego Museum of Man

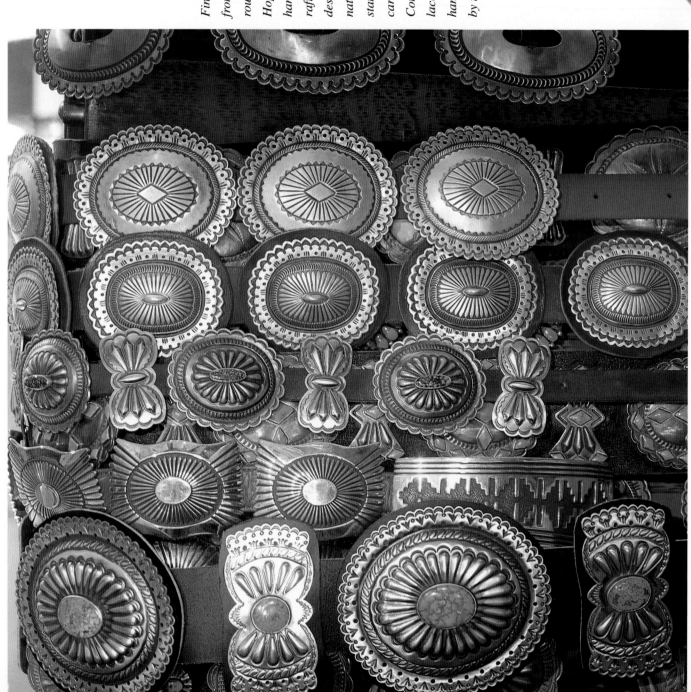

Concho belts

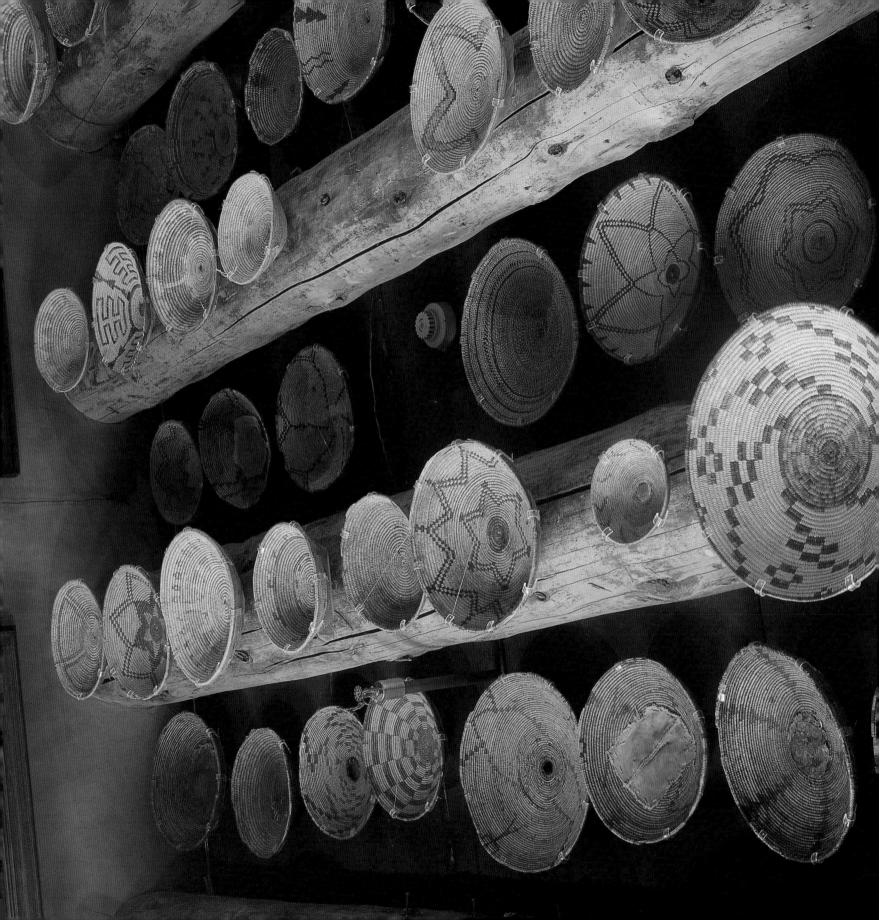

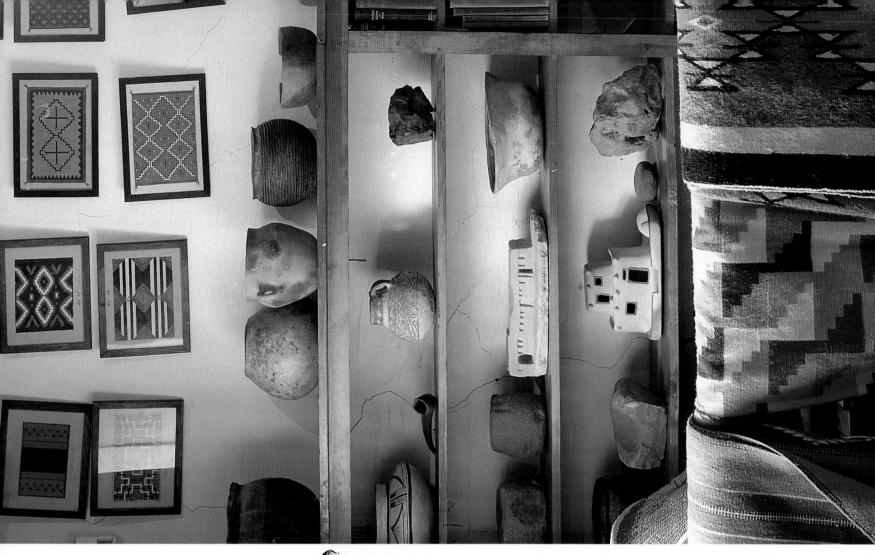

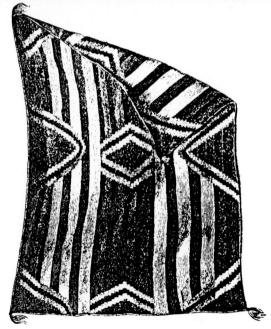

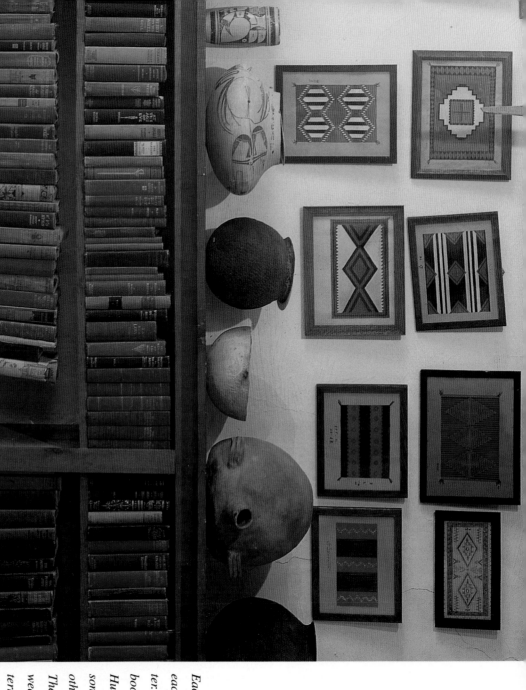

Rug room

Each trading post has a rug room; each rug room has its own character. The small paintings above the bookcases in the rug room at Hubbell are watercolors of designs, some gifts of visiting artists and others commissioned by Hubbell. These might be loaned to new weavers as an inspiration or pattern, or used by visitors who wished to order a custom-made rug.

79

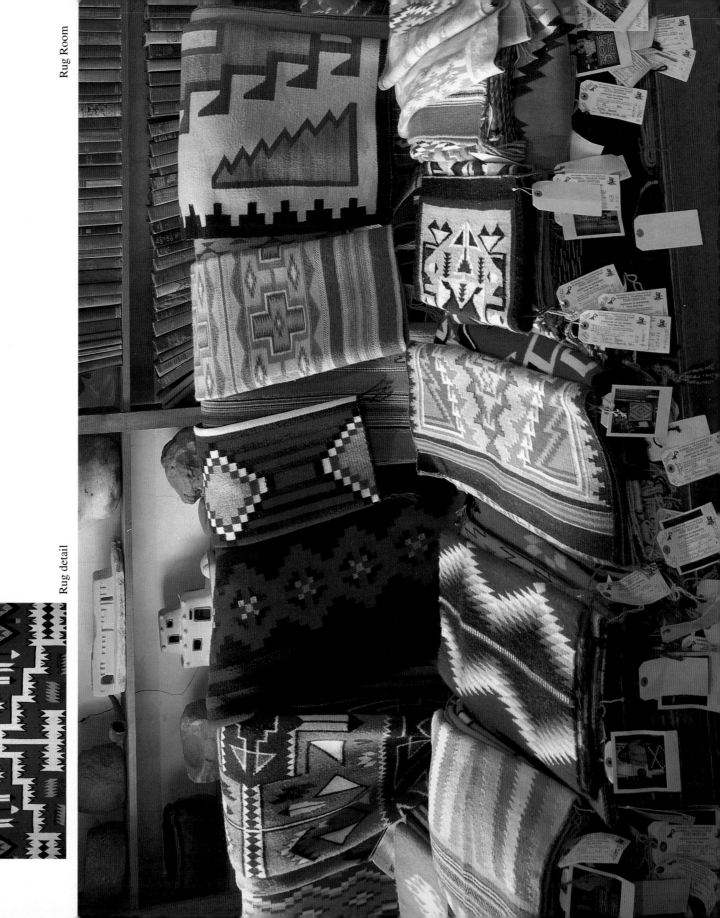

Rug Room

Rug detail

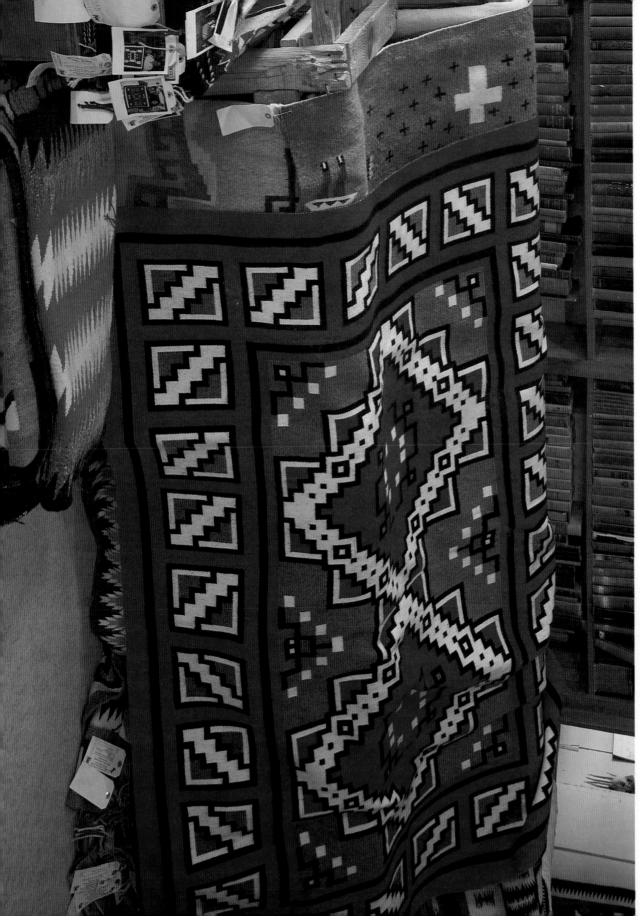

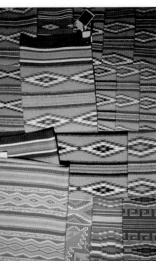

Chinle rugs

THE ARTIST

In the interpretive center at Hubbell, three traditional looms are set up. Each holds the first unfurling of a substantial-sized weaving. The warp strings are ready, looped in a taut figure eight around the warp beam at the top and the web beam at the bottom. The heddle rods are in place, attached by string loops to half of the vertical warp strings, creating the first shed, or passageway for the weft. A batten, which holds the shed open, and a weaving comb, used to pack the weft down tight, lie on the floor near each loom among subtly colored balls of yarn. A few inches of weaving have been completed at the bottom of each loom, giving only a teasing glimpse of the whole pattern held in the weaver's mind.

Tacked to each loom is a photograph of the weaver, a representation of the will behind the idea, the creative force behind the as-yet unrealized weaving. In the trading post rug room here and at all of the posts are stacks of weavings, carefully folded or draped over racks, hanging from the wall or stacked on the floor, jewels of concentrated color and creativity. Each has its

informative manila tag bearing the name of the trading post, the pattern of the rug, and the weaver's name. Though this provenance may be valuable information to the collector, its doesn't begin to tell the story of the rug, of the rug's weaver and how she came to realize her idea.

What compels a weaver to spend the long hours it takes to create a rug: to shear the sheep, carefully selecting the best fleece from the shoulder, flanks, and back; to dig yucca roots for wool soap; to wash and rinse the wool repeatedly after picking out leaves, burrs, and other large contaminants; to card the wool, repeatedly pulling the cards against each other until the fibers are untangled and the wool pulls away in a fluffy roll; to spin the fluffy rolls, or batts, into yarn, using a hand-held spindle, spinning the yarn once, twice, perhaps three times to the desired fineness; to gather roots and berries and other dyestuffs, boil them in steaming vats, and soak the wool several days in each to obtain a range of colors; to set up the warp on the warp frame, carefully looping it, then adjusting it to the proper tension after transferring it to the fixed loom? Hundreds of hours are invested in creating her own materials before the weaving begins. And then to sit at the loom and weave, day in and day out, perhaps under a tree near her hogan, perhaps in an interpretive center or trading post, carrying a vision of the rug in her head, the pattern originally suggested long ago by a trader and modified by her grandmother, her mother, her aunt, before becoming her own unique creation.

Various sources estimate that a traditional rug takes 300 to 500 hours to create, depending on its size, the number of colors, and the intricacy of the pattern. A room-sized rug may take two weavers working together a year to complete. Using aniline dyes instead of natural dyes, or purchasing the commercial yarn available at the trading post, can cut drastically the number of hours spent in preparation. Still, the number of hours at the loom is high and the financial incentive low. What drives the weaver? What keeps her at her loom?

At the Canyon de Chelly Visitor's Center, a silversmith polishes his latest creation, an inlaid bracelet in the Hopi style, on the wheel, then sets it in the display next to several others, all gleaming in the filtered light. Small farms and houses circle one silver band. A band of Kokopellis play flute and dance around the circumference of another. Each tiny figure, cut individually from the metal sheet, has its own character, its own step to the music.

What keeps the silversmith at his work: selecting and grading the turquoise, coral, lapis, quartz; carefully matching color to color; cutting and shaping a stone; making a pattern of bezels and setting a stone in each; carefully arranging an elaborate inlay; stamping and rocking patterns into the metal of a blank concho; biting patterns deeper into the metal with acids; forming the bracelet band to the wrist; burnishing the finished piece so that it gleams in the afternoon sun? What keeps the silversmith at his bench?

What makes us create? What is it in us that rises, bubbles up to the surface, waters the desert of everyday life? What drives us to bring forth beauty, to take textures and colors and shapes, to

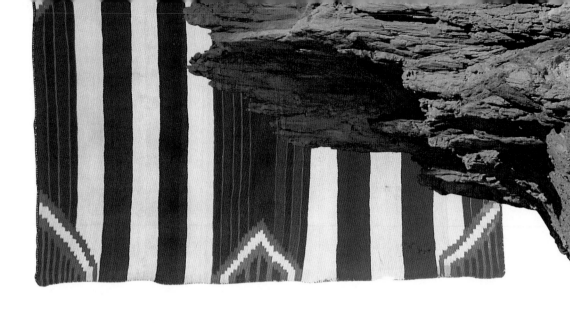

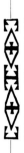

combine these things and transform them into
something else, something greater than their
parts? To spend long hours before the loom or at
the jeweler's bench? To card the wool, to shear
the sheep, to spin the yarn? To polish the stones,
to cut and shape the metal, to twist and braid
wires together, to etch with acids and stamp with
a mark of one's own design?

The casual observer may not see much here to
inspire—acres of rocks and dust and an occasional
stand of trees. But the eye of the artist takes in all:
the miles of open country, of grass baked brown
by the sun, rounded pink and salmon and coral
rocks, cliffs of gray and scarlet, hills of rust-col-
ored earth, hillocks of lumpy gray where no plants
grow; of rabbit brush and wild buckwheat in full
yellow flower, unexpected patches of pine forest,
spectacular sheer-sided canyons whose flat floors
hold meandering streams, meadows where cream-
white sheep fatten all summer; of cliffs where
Kokopelli whirls and plays, where strange, regal
figures with horns, etched into the rock, grow

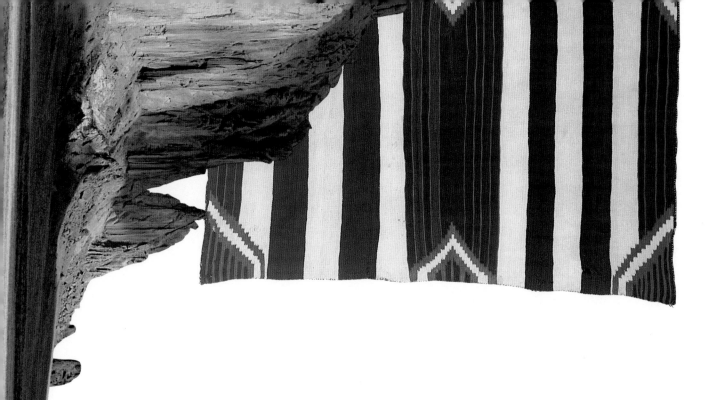

larger in the evening shadows. And over all this mass of sky, rose and apricot at dawn, then the high, thin robin's egg of midday that deepens as the shadows lengthen to wrap all in midnight blue. The eye of the artist takes in all, draws inspiration from the rocks, the open places, the spectacular pinnacles and spires, the earth itself. The patterns written into the bed of a wash by rushing water. The twisted branches of a pinyon pine. The summer lightning, forking down.

Writing has been described as a conversation with one's self. Weaving, indeed any creative act, may spring from that same place, that ongoing dialog with the self, that impulse both to explain the self and to endure beyond it. A young woman learns to weave at her mother's side, starting first by carding wool, then progressing to making small weavings, pillow tops and such, until she is a weaver in her own right, teaching other young weavers. A legacy, made of the best things in us. A striving toward beauty. A Tree of Life bursting into impossibly radiant bloom in the desert of the Southwest.

Phase III chief blanket, 1870–1880, courtesy San Diego Museum of Man; Shiprock, New Mexico

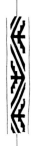

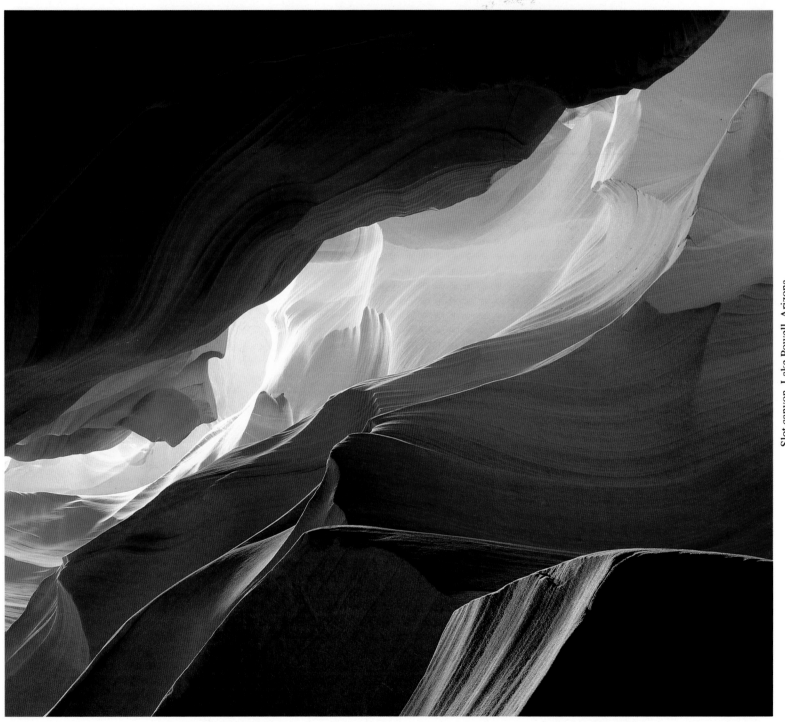

Slot canyon, Lake Powell, Arizona

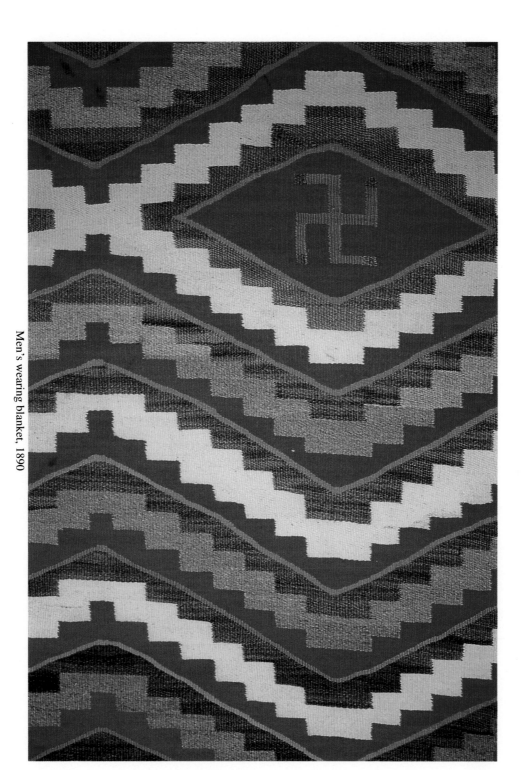

Men's wearing blanket, 1890

Navajo rugs incorporate the colors of nature—the vermilion of the cliffs, the cream-white of undyed wool, the grays of basalt and dust. Their crackling energy is pulled from the weather, the sky, the jagged rocks. The swastika design incorporated into this rug fell into disuse after its adoption and subsequent debasement by the Nazi Party. ◇

87

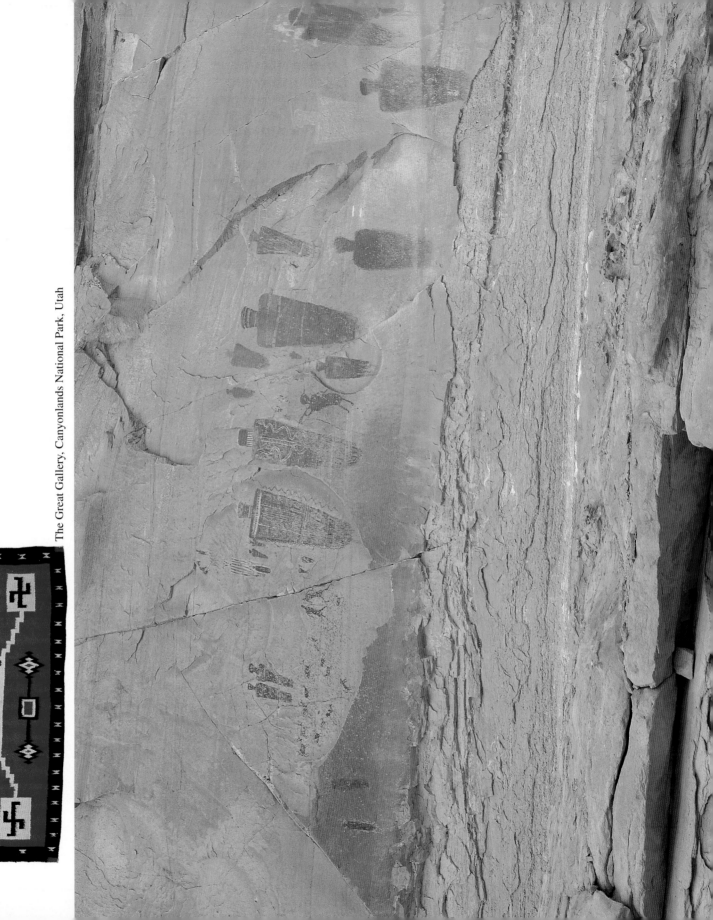

The Great Gallery, Canyonlands National Park, Utah

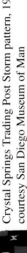

Crystal Springs Trading Post Storm pattern, 1900,
courtesy San Diego Museum of Man

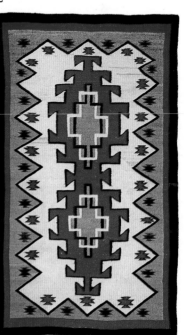

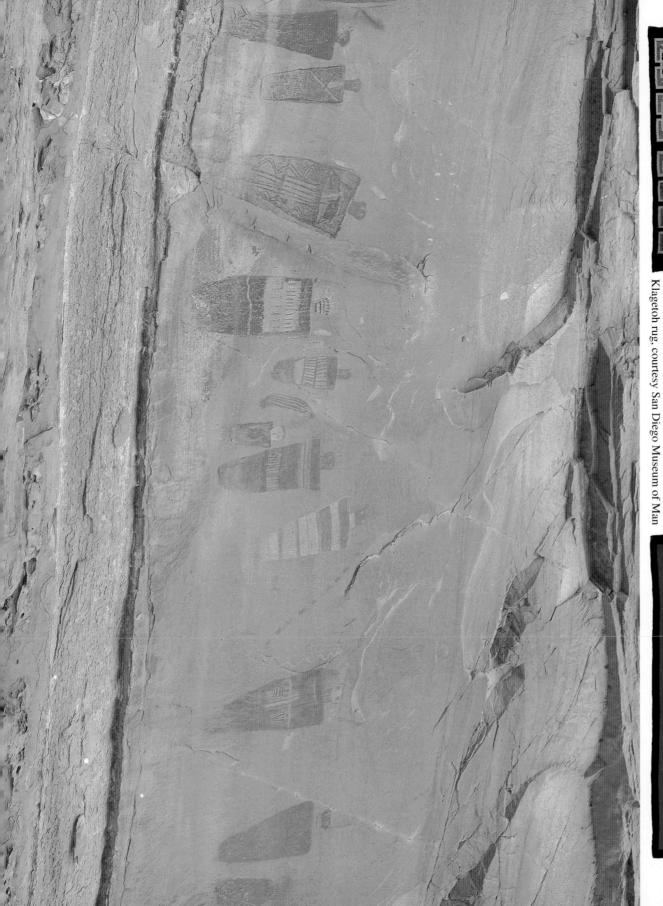

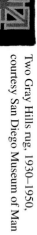

Two Gray Hills rug, 1930–1950, courtesy San Diego Museum of Man

Klagetoh rug, courtesy San Diego Museum of Man

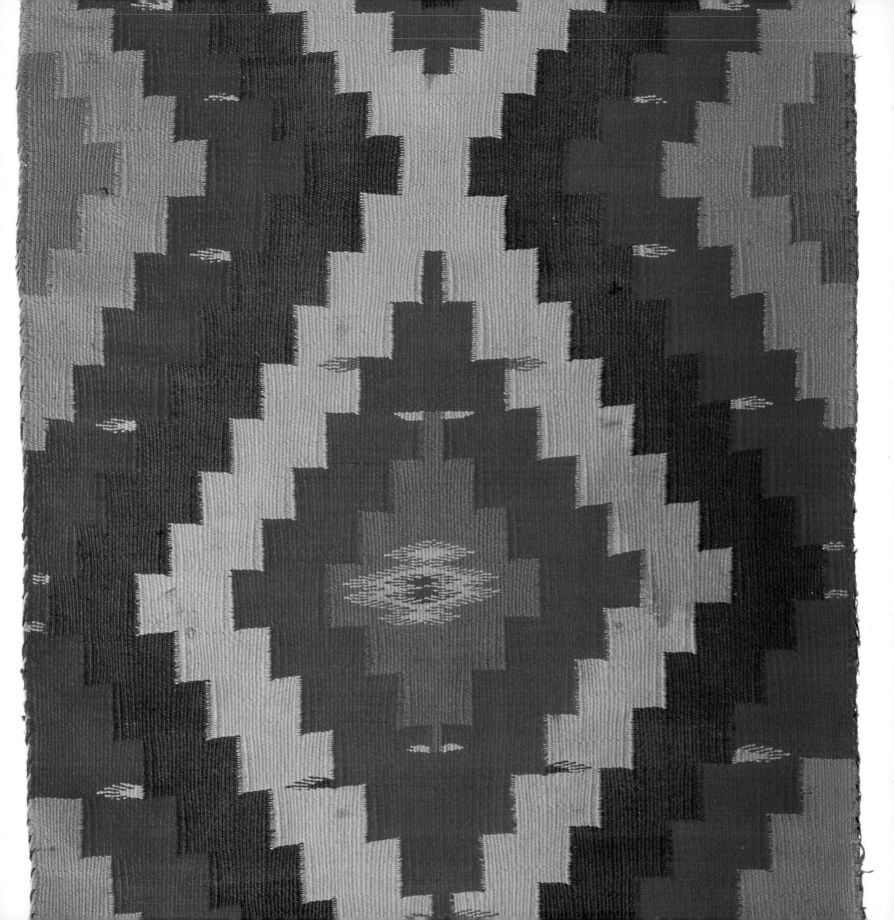

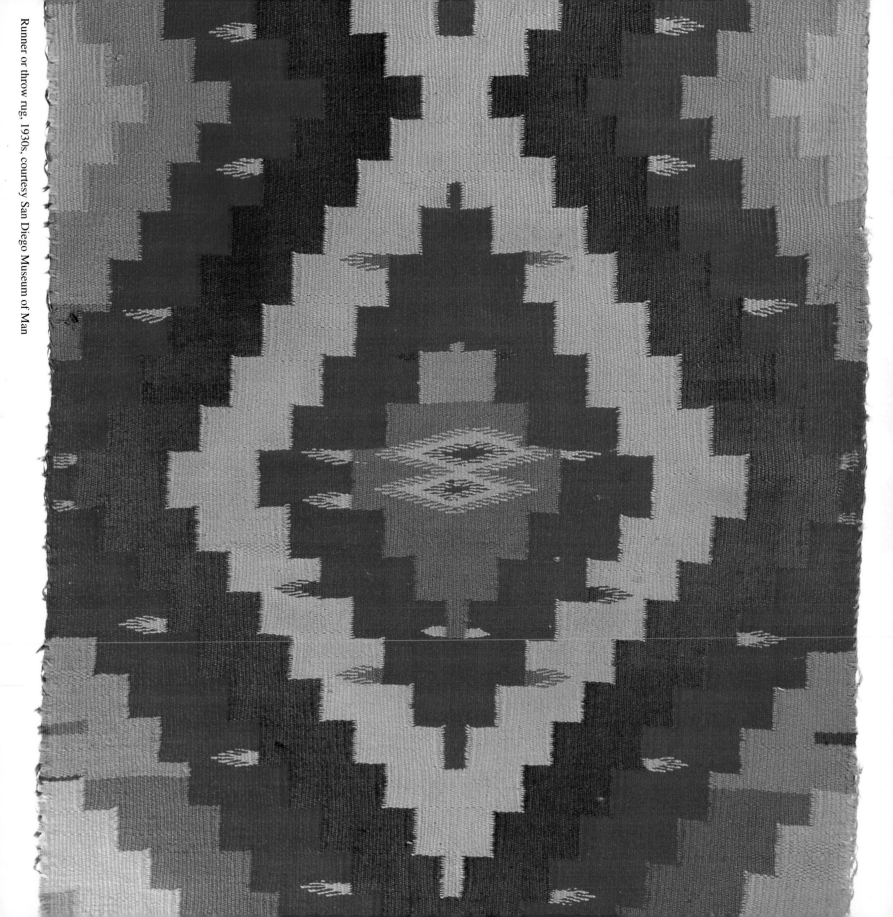

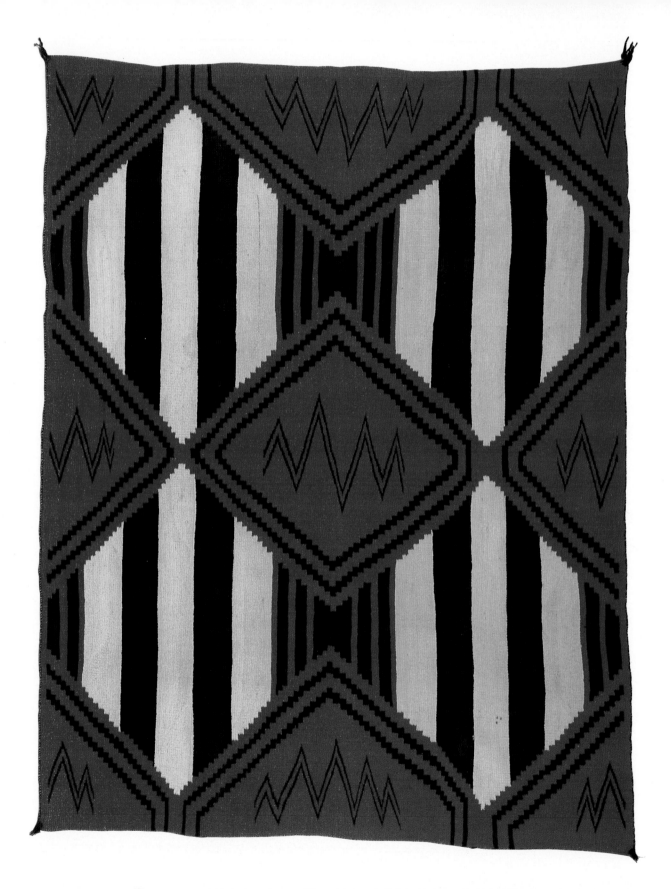

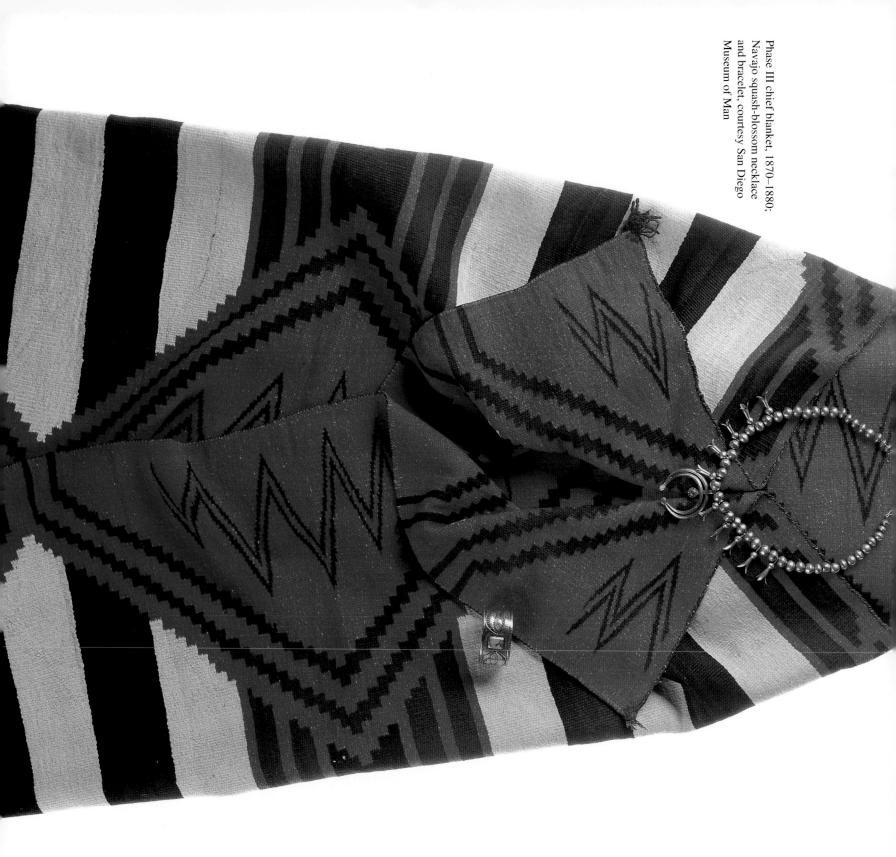

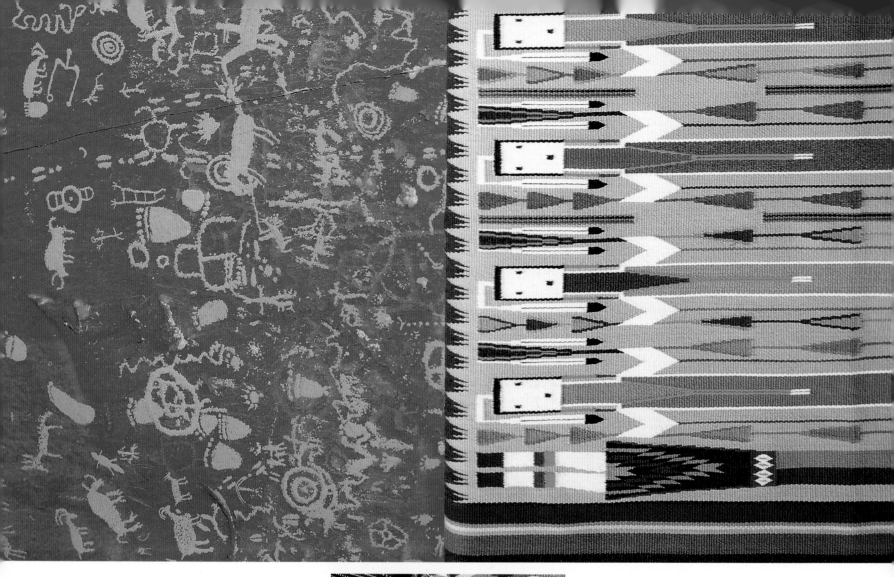

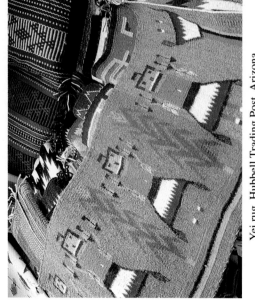

Yei rug, Hubbell Trading Post, Arizona

The Yei, supernatural and unpredictable beings who control Navajo destiny, are often depicted on rugs from the Ship Rock and Lukachukai areas. The elongated, stylized figures are often shown holding rattles or pine boughs. Oftentimes a Rainbow Guardian is stretched around three sides of the rug, leaving an opening on the eastern side. Supernatural beings may also be represented in the rock art spread far and wide across the Southwest, although many interpretations have been suggested. Whether their meaning is concrete or abstract, spiritual or practical, they are powerful reminders of their vanished makers.

Yei rug by Ella Peacock, courtesy Lema's Trading Post; ancient petroglyphs

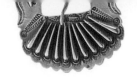

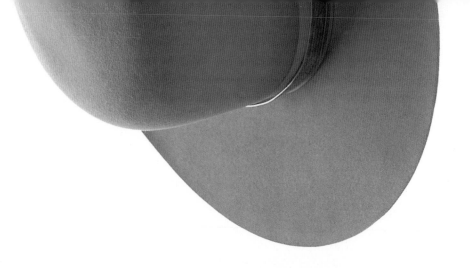

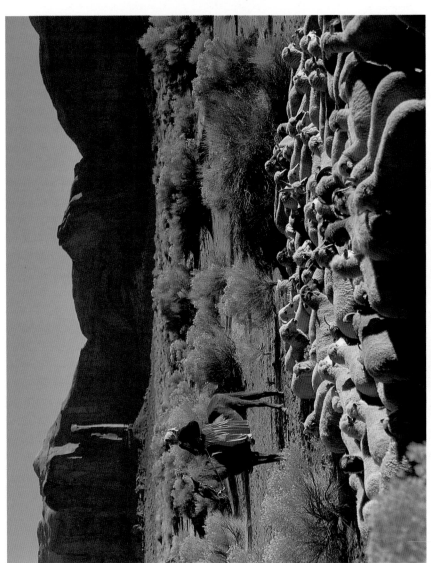

Sheep and herder, Monument Valley, Arizona–Utah

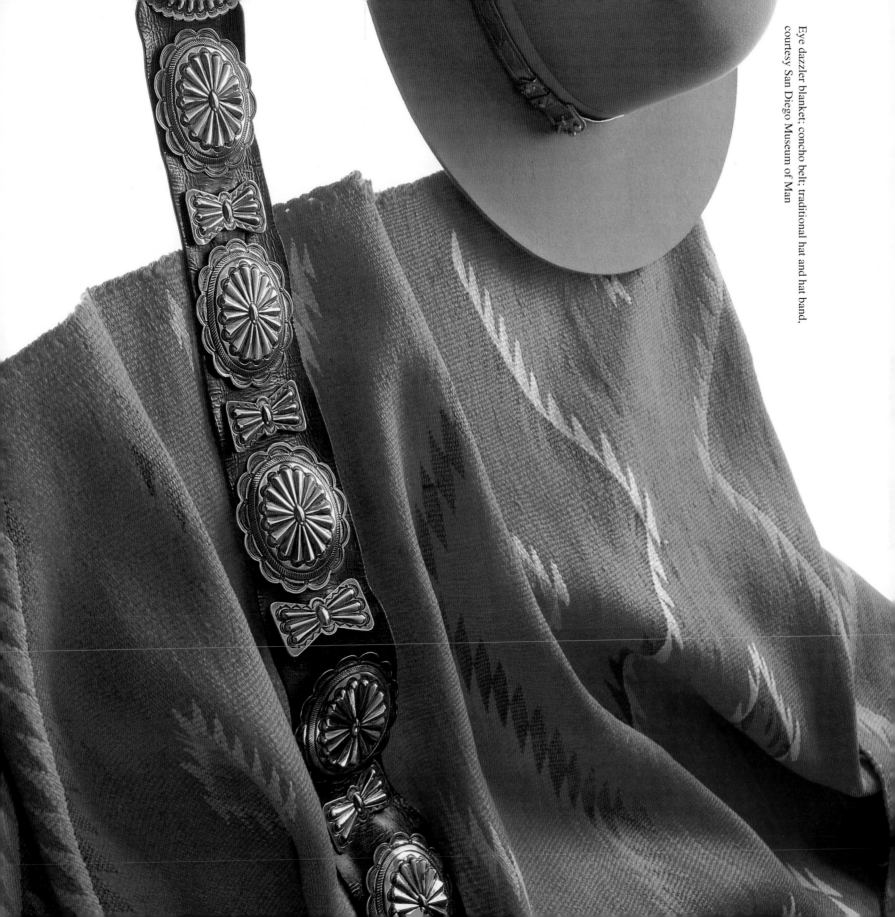

Eye dazzler blanket; concho belt; traditional hat and hat band, courtesy San Diego Museum of Man

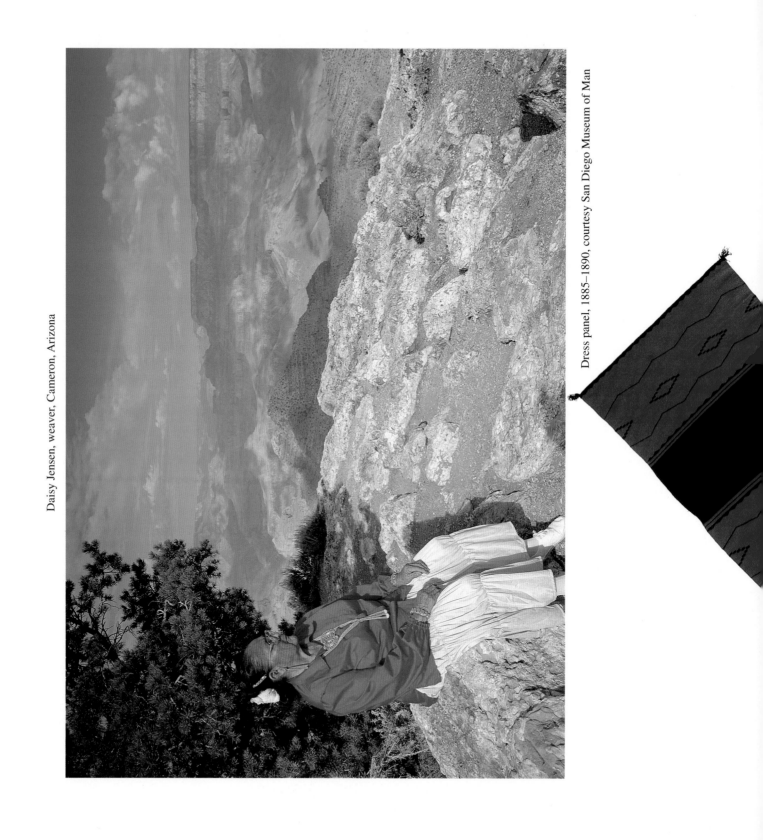

Daisy Jensen, weaver, Cameron, Arizona

Dress panel, 1885–1890, courtesy San Diego Museum of Man

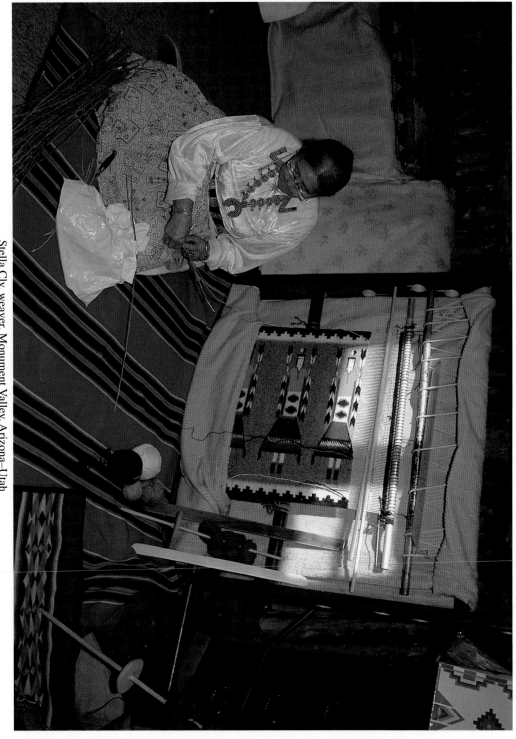

Stella Cly, weaver, Monument Valley, Arizona–Utah

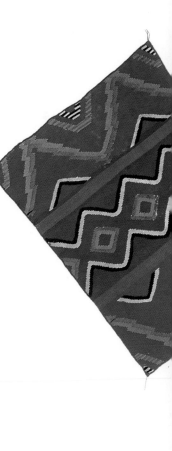

Child's wearing blanket, 1870, courtesy San Diego Museum of Man

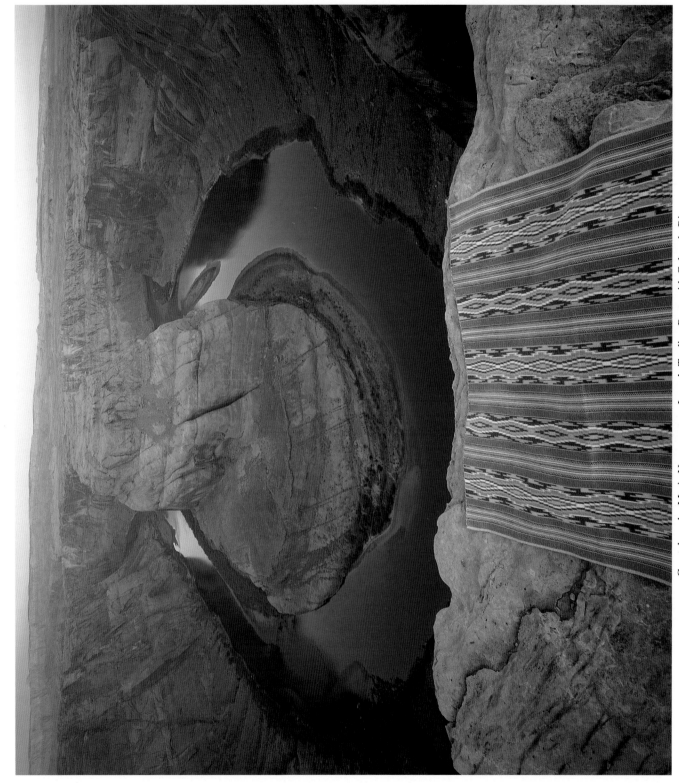

Crystal rug by Marie Nez, courtesy Lema's Trading Post, with Colorado River

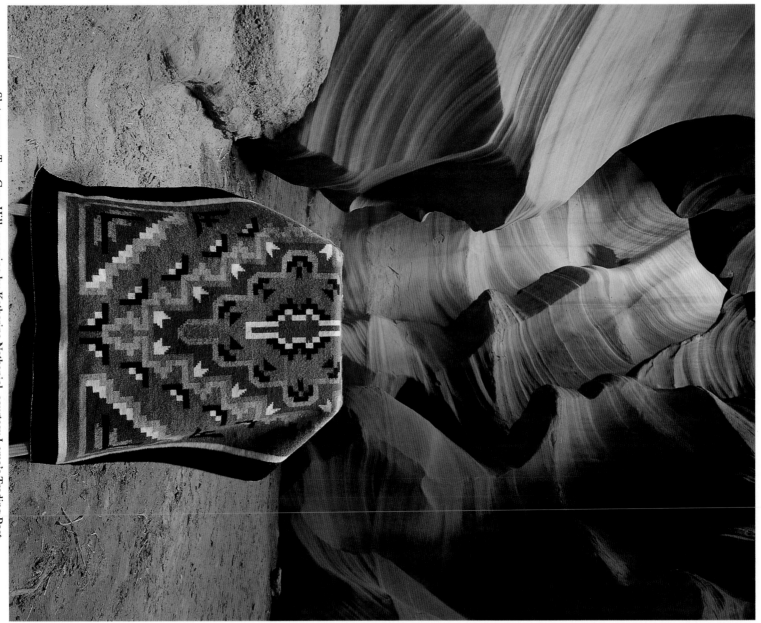

Slot canyon; Two Gray Hills weaving by Katherine Nathaniel, courtesy Lema's Trading Post

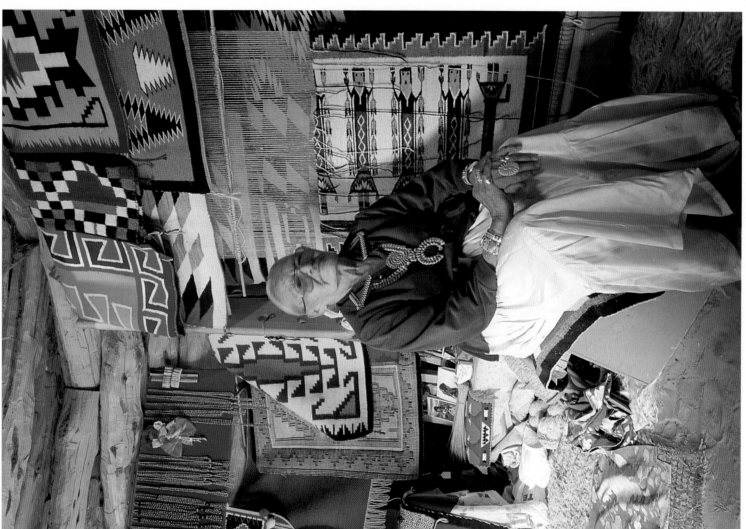

What of the weaver? She spins her web alone, surrounded by the magnificence of nature or by the six walls of her hogan. She works in the confines of an interpretive center or a trading post, in contact with others, but alone with her design. The Navajo woman weaves in harmony and walks in beauty.

Susie Yazzie, weaver, Monument Valley, Arizona

Saddle blanket, 1890, courtesy
San Diego Museum of Man

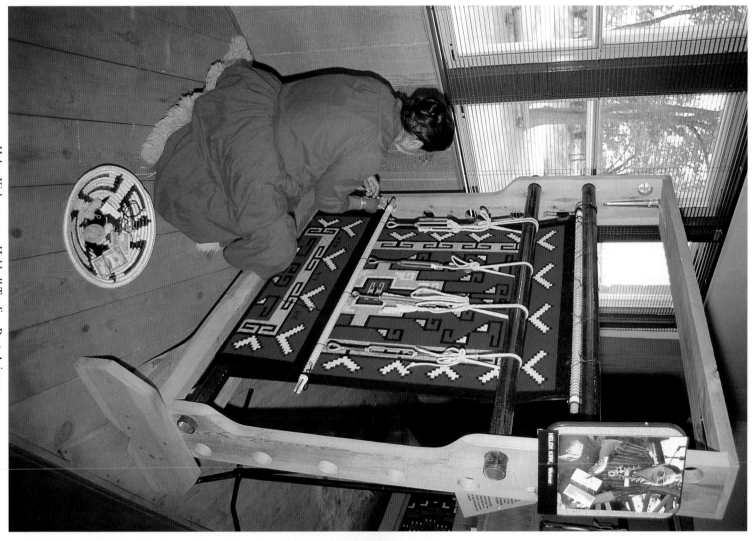

Helen Kirk, weaver, Hubbell Trading Post, Arizona

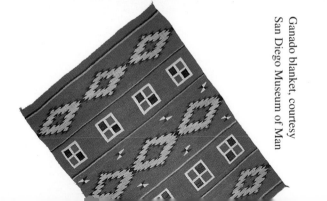

Ganado blanket, courtesy
San Diego Museum of Man

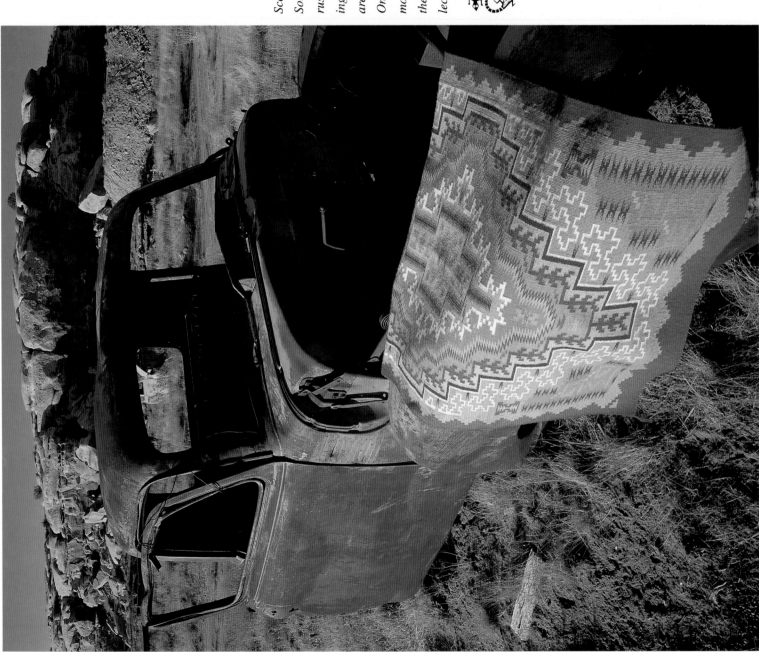

Scattered throughout the Southwest are abandoned vehicles, rusting relics of the past, tantalizing to the classic car lover. Most are still valued by their owners. One old desert garage contained more than 150 cars dating from the 1920s; unfortunately for collectors, none were for sale.

Burntwater rug by Bertha Roan, courtesy Lema's Trading Post; old Chevy

104

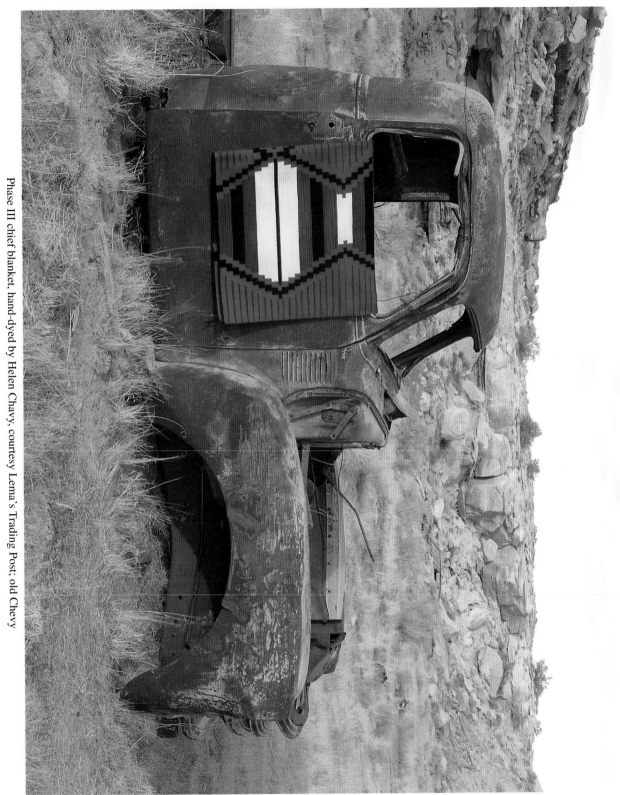

Phase III chief blanket, hand-dyed by Helen Chavy, courtesy Lema's Trading Post; old Chevy

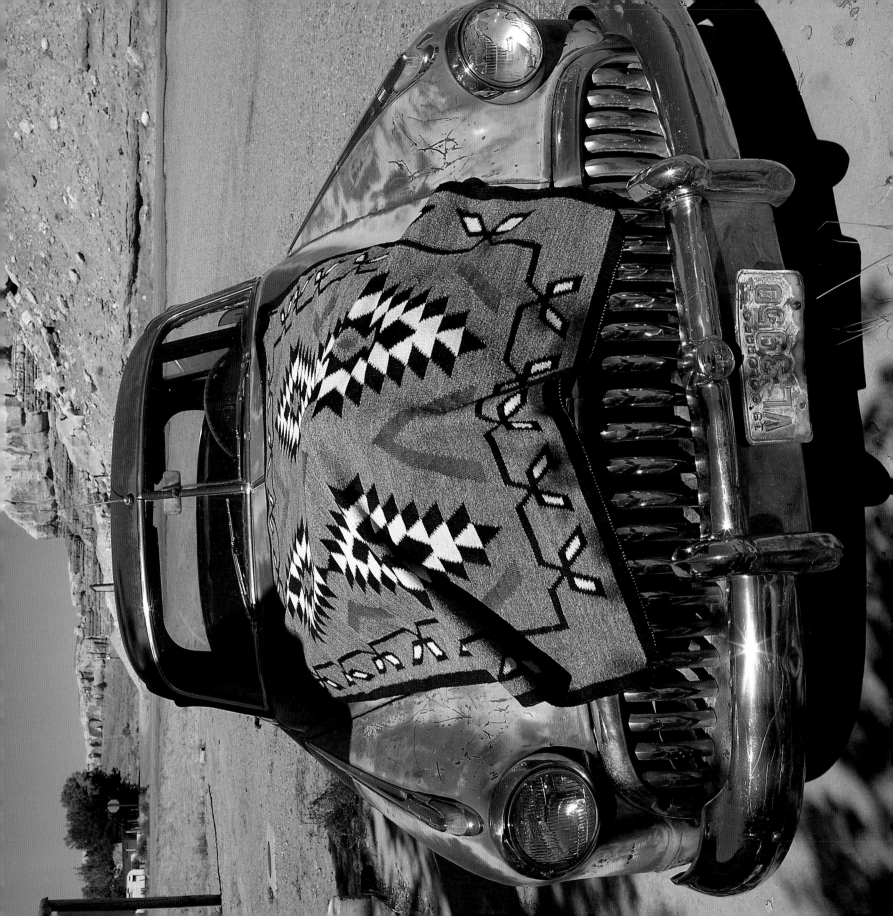

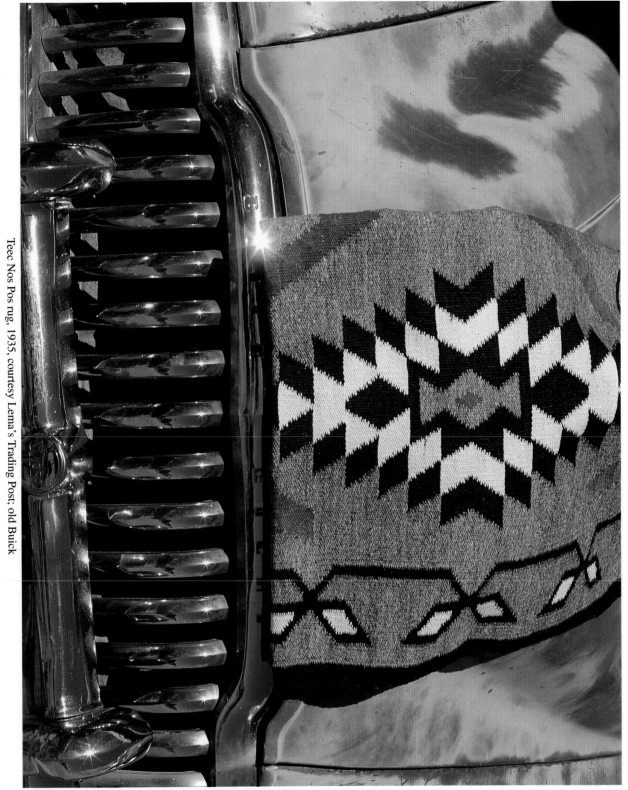

Teec Nos Pos rug, 1935, courtesy Lema's Trading Post; old Buick

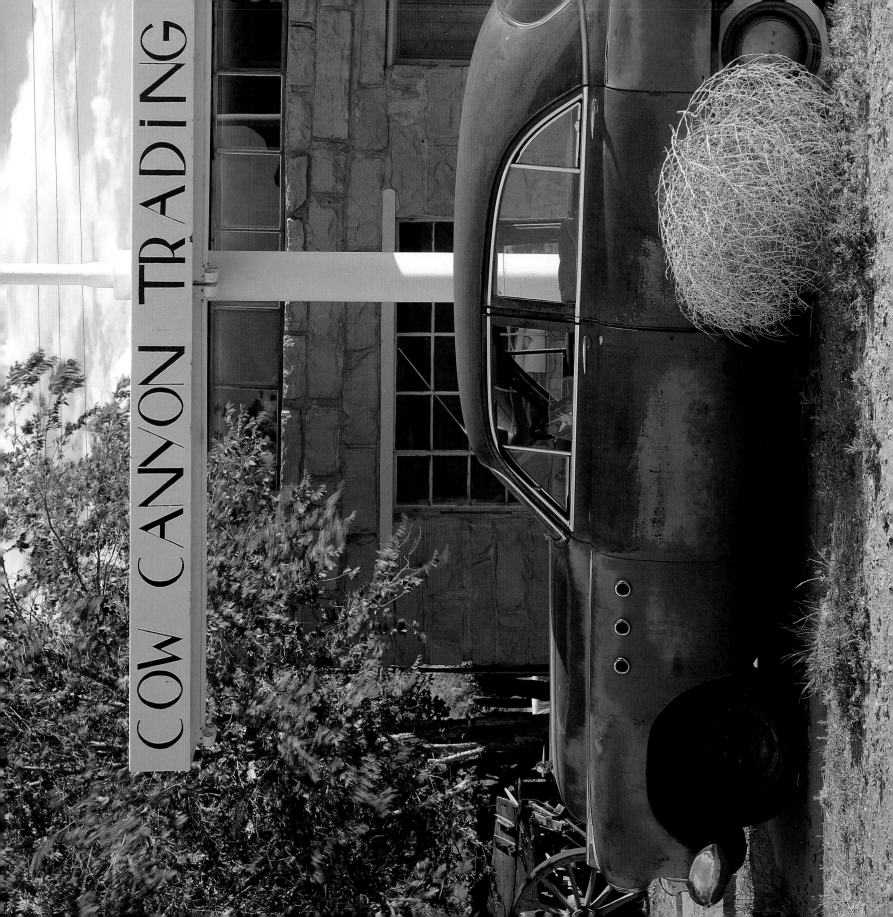

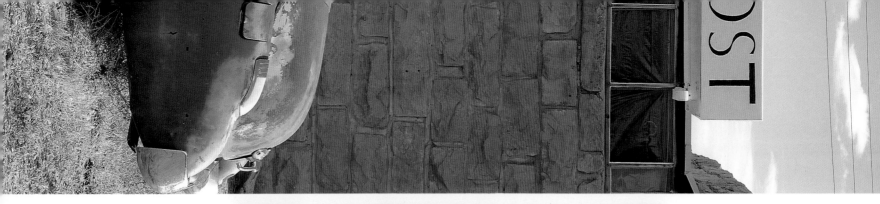

Cow Canyon Trading Post, New Mexico; old Buick

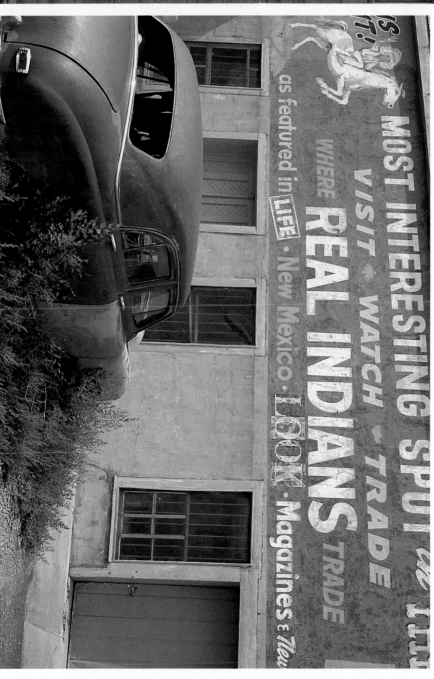

Santo Domingo Trading Post, New Mexico; old Plymouth

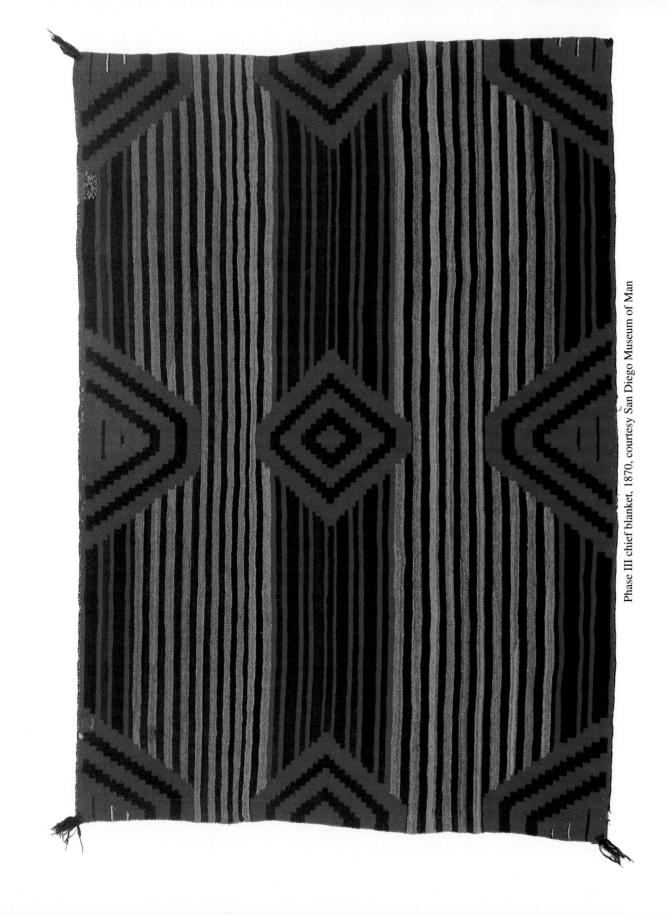

Phase III chief blanket, 1870, courtesy San Diego Museum of Man

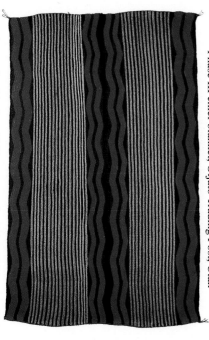

Women's wearing blanket, 1850, courtesy San Diego Museum of Man

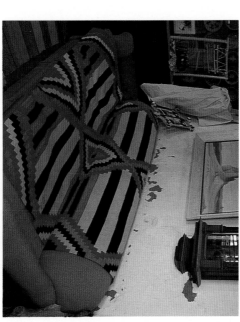

Phase III chief blanket, Oljato Trading Post, Utah

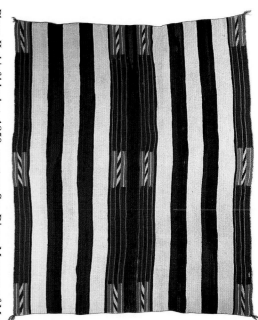

Phase II chief blanket, 1850, courtesy San Diego Museum of Man

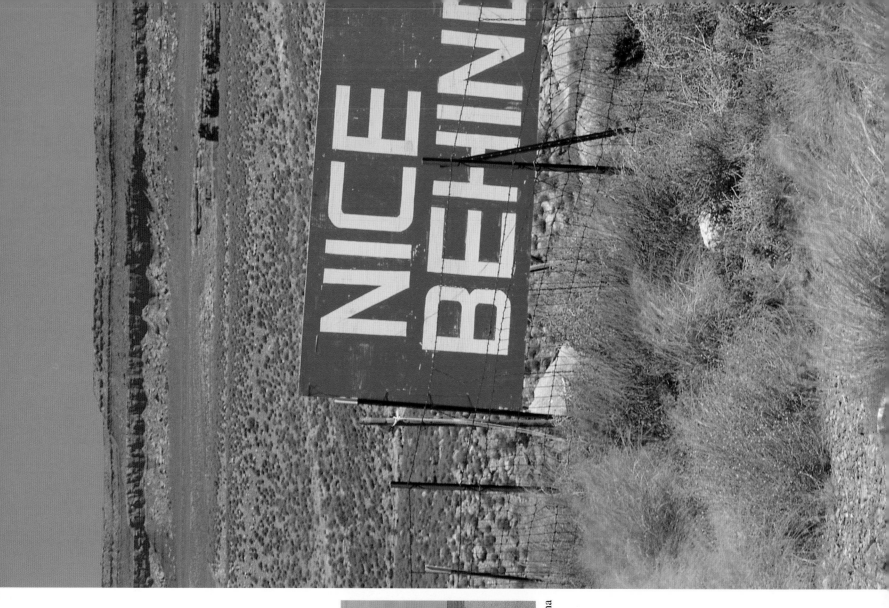

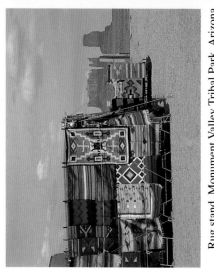

Rug stand, Monument Valley Tribal Park, Arizona

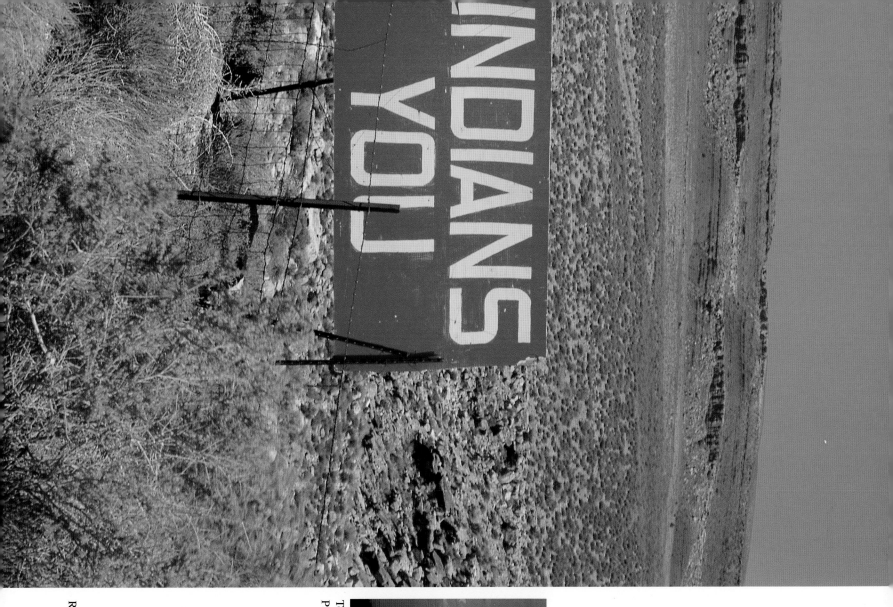

Rug stand sign, Navajo reservation, Arizona

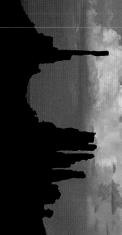

Totem Pole Rock, Monument Valley Tribal
Park, Arizona

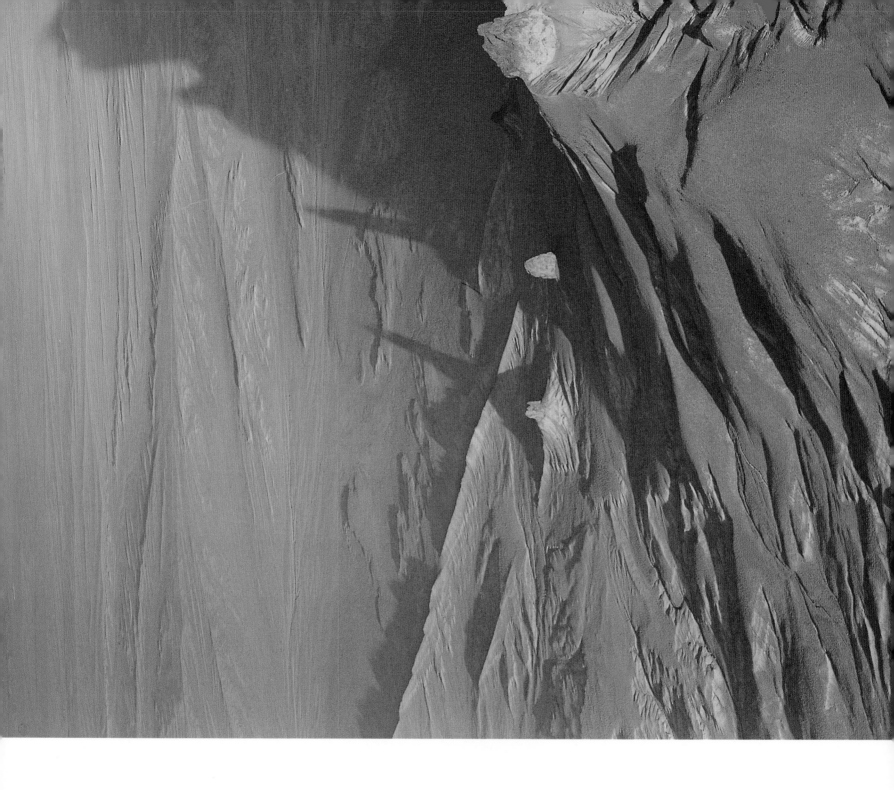

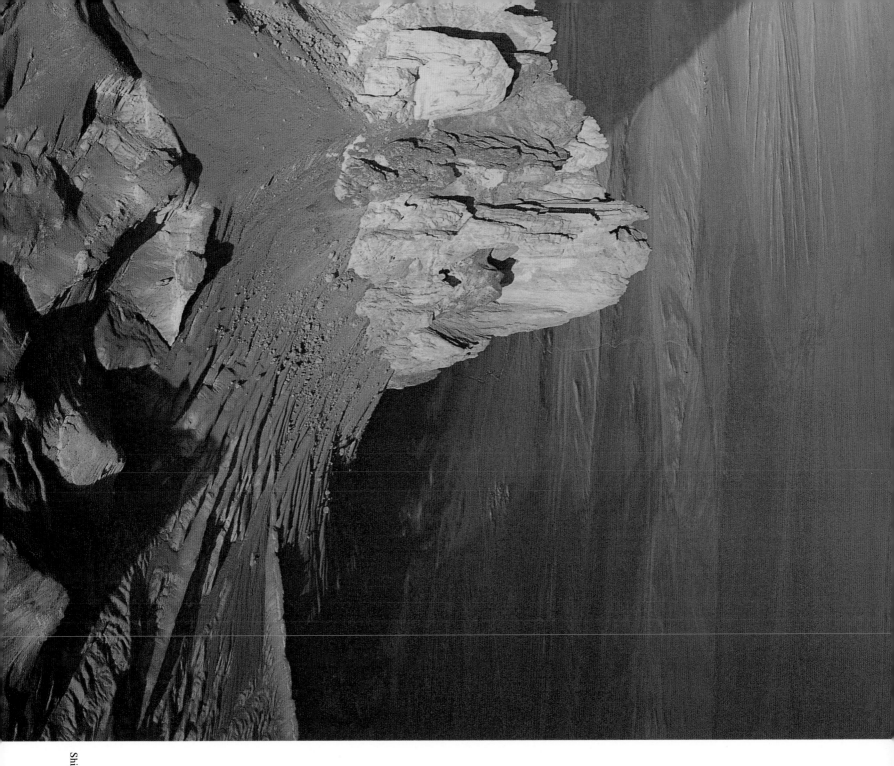

Ship Rock, New Mexico

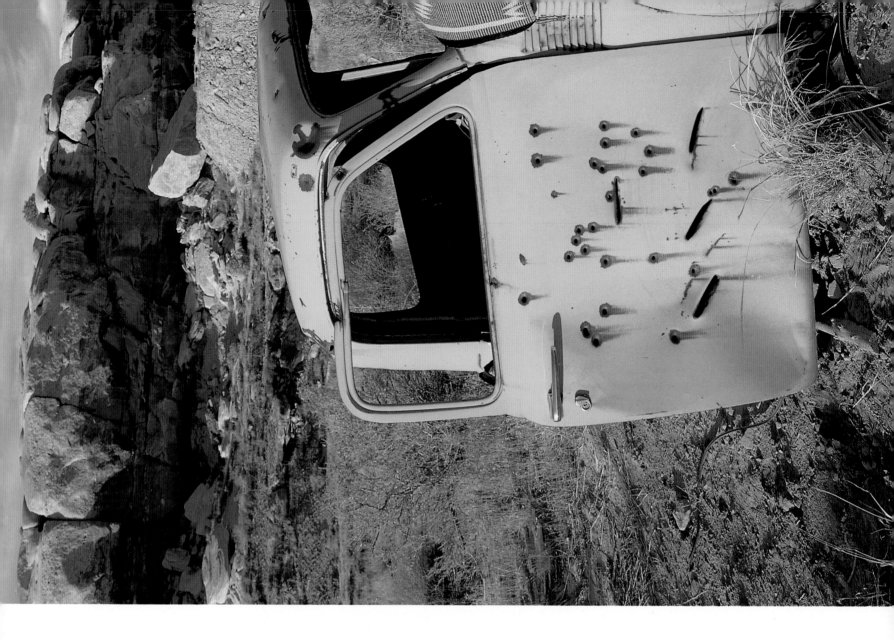

Raised-outline eye dazzler rug by Mae Smith,
courtesy Lema's Trading Post; old Chevy

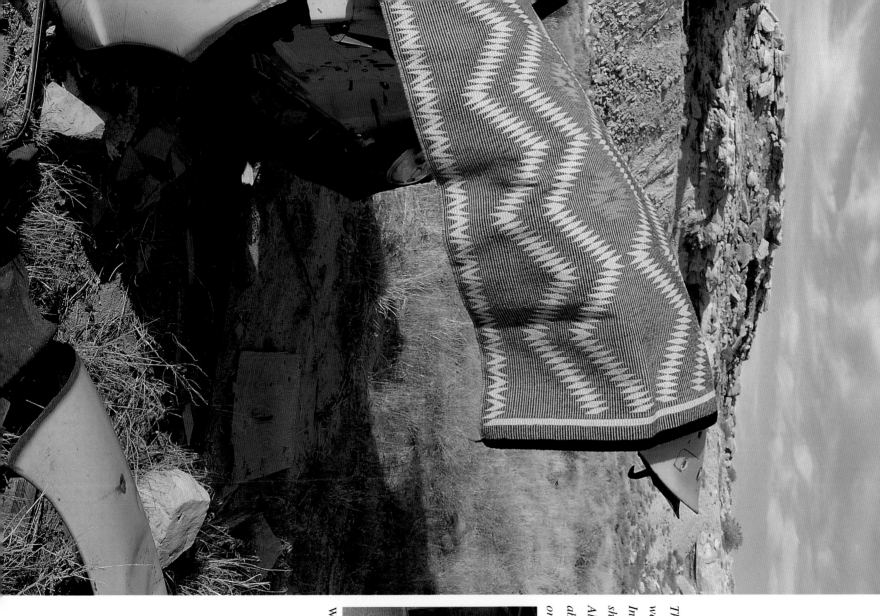

The early traders traveled by horse-drawn wagon, a practice eagerly adopted by the Indians. In time the wagons were given up for shiny, new trucks, purchased in Flagstaff and Albuquerque. As these wore out they were also abandoned, left to become targets for bullets— or cameras.

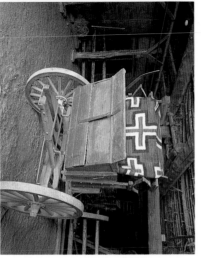

Wagon; Ganado rug, 1895

117

BIBLIOGRAPHY

Babcock, Barbara A. *The Pueblo Storytellers.* Tucson, AZ, and London: University of Arizona Press, 1986.

Brafford, C. J. and Laine Thom. *Dancing Colors: Paths of Native American Women.* San Francisco: Chronicle Books, 1992.

Bruchac, Joseph. *Native American Stories.* Golden, CO: Fulcrum Publishing, 1991.

Brugge, David M. *Hubbell Trading Post: National Historic Site.* Tucson, AZ: Southwest Parks and Monuments Association, 1993.

Brugge, David M. *Navajos in the Catholic Church Records of New Mexico: 1694–1875.* Tsaile, AZ: Navajo Community College Press, 1985.

Burland, Cottie. *North American Indian Mythology.* Revised by Marion Wood. New York: Pater Bedrick Books, 1985.

Caduto, Michael J., and Joseph Bruchac. *Keepers of the Earth.* Golden, CO: Fulcrum Publishing, 1988.

Colton, Harold S. *Hopi Kachina Dolls: With a Key to Their Identification.* Albuquerque, NM: University of New Mexico Press, 1987.

Campbell, Tyrone, Joel Kopp, and Kate Kopp. *Navajo Pictorial Weaving, 1880–1950.* New York: Dutton Studio Books, 1991.

Chronic, Halka. *Roadside Geology of Arizona.* Missoula, MT: Mountain Press, 1983.

Courlander, Harold. *The Fourth World of the Hopis.* Albuquerque, NM: University of New Mexico Press, 1971.

Davis, Barbara A. *Edward S. Curtis: The Life and Times of a Shadow Catcher.* San Francisco: Chronicle Books, 1985.

Erickson, John T. *Kachinas: An Evolving Hopi Art Form?* Phoenix, AZ: Heard Museum, 1977.

Fowler, Dan D. *In a Sacred Manner We Live.* Barre, MA: Barre Publishers, 1972.

Grant, Michael. *American Southwest: A People and Their Landscape.* San Diego, CA: Thunder Bay Press, 1992.

Hegemann, Elizabeth Compton. *Navaho Trading Days.* Albuquerque, NM: University of New Mexico Press, 1963.

Hooker, Kathy E. *Time among the Navajo: Traditional Lifeways on the Reservation.* Santa Fe: Museum of New Mexico Press, 1991.

Houlihan, Collings, Nestor, and Batkin. *Harmony by Hand: Art of the Southwest Indians; Basketry, Weaving, Pottery.* San Francisco: Chronicle Books, 1987.

James, H. L. *Rugs and Posts.* West Chester, PA: Schifter Publishing, 1988.

Lamb, Susan. *A Guide to Navajo Rugs.* Tucson, AZ: Southwest Parks and Monuments Association, 1992.

Laubin, Reginald, and Gladys Laubin. *Indian Dances of North America.* Norman, OK, and London: University of Oklahoma Press, 1977.

Lindig, Wolfgang. *Navajo: Tradition and Change in the Southwest.* New York: Facts on File, 1991.

Long, Robert A., and Rose Houk. *Dawn of the Dinosaurs: The Triassic in Petrified Forest.* Petrified Forest, AZ: Petrified Forest Museum Association, 1988.

McQuiston, Don, and Debra McQuiston. *Dolls & Toys of Native America: A Journey through Childhood.* San Francisco: Chronicle Books, 1995.

Niethammer, Carolyn. *Daughters of the Earth: The Lives and Keepers of American Indian Women.* London: Collier MacMillan Publishers, 1977.

Noble, David Grant. *Houses Beneath the Rock: The Anasazi of Canyon de Chelly and Navajo National Monument.* Santa Fe, NM: Ancient City Press, 1986.

Pike, Donald R. *Anasazi: Ancient People of the Rock.* New York: Crown Publishers, 1974.

Richardson, Fleming, Paula Lushy, and Judith Lynn. *Grand Endeavors of American Indian Photography.* Washington, DC: Smithsonian Institution Press, 1993.

Roessel, Robert, Jr. *A Pictorial History of the Navajo from 1860 to 1910.* Rough Rock, AZ: Navajo Curriculum Center, 1980.

Schmidt, Jeremy. *In the Spirit of Mother Earth: Nature in Native American Art.* San Francisco: Chronicle Books, 1994.

Spencer, Robert, et al. *The Native Americans.* New York: Harper and Row, 1965.

Stokes, William Lee. *Scenes of the Plateau Lands and How They Came to Be.* Salt Lake City, UT: Starstone Publishing Company, 1969.

Taylor, Colin P., and William C. Sturtevant. *The Native Americans: The Indigenous People of North America.* New York: Salamander Books, 1991.

Thom, Laine. *Becoming Brave: The Path to Native American Manhood.* San Francisco: Chronicle Books, 1992.

Viele, Catherine W. *Navajo National Monument.* Tucson, AZ: Southwest Parks and Monuments Association, 1993.

Walter, Anna Lee. *The Spirit of Native America: Beauty and Mysticism in American Indian Art.* San Francisco: Chronicle Books, 1989.

Webb, William, and Robert A. Weinstein. *Dwellers at the Source: Southwestern Indian Photographs of A. C. Vroman, 1895–1904.* New York: Grossman, 1973.

Acknowledgments

Produced by McQuiston & McQuiston; artifact photography by John Oldenkamp and coordinated by Grace Johnson; scenic photography by Tom Till; composition by ColorType; printed by South Sea International Press.

Special thanks should be given to the staff of the San Diego Museum of Man: Grace Johnson, Curator, Stephanie Salfield, Curator, and Ken Hedges, Chief Curator. Without their assistance this book could not have been published. Additional thanks are due to the kind staff at Hubbell Trading Post National Historic Site, Cameron Trading Post, and Lema's Trading Post.